WILLIAM AND KATE'S
BRITAIN

An Insider's Guide to the Haunts of the Duke and Duchess of Cambridge

Splendid
PUBLICATIONS

WILLIAM AND KATE'S
BRITAIN

An Insider's Guide to the Haunts of the Duke and Duchess of Cambridge

Claudia Joseph

To Oliver, Hal and Nathan…may you travel far

William and Kate's Britain
An Insider's Guide to the Haunts of the Duke and Duchess of Cambridge

Written by Claudia Joseph

Splendid Publications Ltd
Unit 7
Twin Bridges Business Park
South Croydon
Surrey CR2 6PL

www.splendidpublications.co.uk

British Library Cataloguing in Publication Data is available from The British Library

ISBN: 9781909109650

Designed by Chris Fulcher at Swerve Creative Design & Marketing Ltd.
www.swerve-creative.co.uk

Printed by PPG Print, Portsmouth.

Every effort has been made to fulfil requirements with regard to reproducing copyright material. The author and publisher will be glad to rectify any omissions at the earliest opportunity. Although extensive checks have been made to ensure that all details contained in this book are correct at the time of going to press, readers may wish to confirm directions and opening times before setting out on a long journey.

CONTENTS

LONDON & GREATER LONDON 65

EAST OF ENGLAND 127

EAST MIDLANDS 145

WEST MIDLANDS 151

INTRODUCTION

They are the most celebrated couple in Britain: when Prince William wed Kate Middleton at Westminster Abbey, millions tuned in, the Royal Mint produced an official coin and merchandisers went into overdrive. Now, readers of William and Kate's Britain can follow in the Duke and Duchess of Cambridge's footsteps and visit some of their favourite haunts. Perhaps you want to tour Britain's royal palaces, visit its stunning castles or see its picturesque churches? Why not visit William and Kate's favourite restaurants and shops, have a pint in their local pubs or stay in the hotels they have frequented? You can explore the towns and villages where they grew up, discover where they went to school and see the military colleges and bases where William has served. And for lovers of the countryside, what could be better than a stroll in one of their favourite parks? Whether you are a royal watcher, history lover or tourist – or simply interested in Britain's rich heritage – delve into this unique guide to the British Isles and discover the secrets of William and Kate's Britain.

Above left: Kate's christening at St Andrew's Church, Bradfield. Middle: William and Kate open Jimmy's new homeless shelter in Cambridge. Right: William launches his Junior Prince's Award at Goole Academy.

SOUTH WEST

CORNWALL

FALMOUTH

The Chain Locker and Shipwrights Pub, Quay Street, Falmouth, Cornwall TR11 3HH

The second oldest pub in Falmouth, which was established in 1660, and is decorated with nautical paraphernalia, proved the obvious venue for Prince William's rower friend Oliver Hicks to celebrate his solo voyage across the Atlantic. So locals were thrilled when William turned up to celebrate. Oliver, a 23-year-old Old Harrovian, spent 124 days out at sea in 2005 in a 23ft boat, travelling 4,040 miles from North America to the Isles of Scilly, becoming the first person to row solo eastwards across the Atlantic as well as the youngest person to complete a solo row across an ocean. 'There was masses of scrummage on the pontoon when I rowed in,' he said afterwards. 'Richard Branson – one of my sponsors – shook my hand and sprayed me with champagne. Willy came along and pulled my hat down over my eyes and then they carried me off to the pub.'

PADSTOW

The National Lobster Hatchery, South Quay, Padstow, Cornwall PL28 8BL

'One lucky little lobster here has been adopted by royalty,' trumpeted The National Lobster Hatchery after the Duke of Edinburgh bought Prince George a crustacean. Prince Philip adopted the creature for his great-grandson when visiting the pioneering marine conservation, research and educational charity, in 2014. He was given a tour of the visitors' centre, met local fishermen and went into Stein's Fisheries, a shop owned by celebrity chef Rick Stein, which sells fresh fish and lobsters. Prince George, who has been sent a £2.50 'Adopt-a-Lobster' certificate, is now receiving regular updates on the creature's progress. The National Lobster Hatchery aims to help conserve the 'vulnerable lobster populations' and 'preserve coastal marine biodiversity' in order to safeguard the livelihoods of small coastal communities and preserve our rich coastal heritage.

Previous page: St Nicholas' Church, Cherington. Top: The Chain Locker and Shipwrights Pub. Above: The National Lobster Hatchery.

DEVON

DARTMOUTH

Britannia Royal Naval College, College Way, Dartmouth, Devon TQ6 0HJ

When Sub Lieutenant William Wales arrived at the Britannia Royal Naval College for a two-month attachment to the Royal Navy in 2008, he was the latest in a long line of royals, beginning with his great-great-grandfather George V, to be cadets at the college. His great-grandfather George VI also trained there, as did the Duke of Edinburgh, who fought at sea during the Second World War and is believed to have met the Queen in Dartmouth. William's uncle Prince Andrew trained at the college before becoming a helicopter pilot in the Falklands War and Prince Charles was there before his service in the Royal Navy, during which he commanded a minehunter. During his first three weeks William studied naval history and learned seamanship, trained alongside the Royal Marines on amphibious and mountain-welfare exercises, dived on a nuclear submarine and flew in all of the navy helicopters, including the Sea Harrier, the Lynx, the Sea King and the Merlin. On his first exercise, he was shown how to handle a 15-metre twin-engine picket boat on the River Dart. Wearing No. 4 dress, the navy's version of combats, he took his turn to drop anchor on the harbour training ship Hindostan, a former minesweeper moored nearby. When he failed a bet to do it first time, he turned to his seven classmates and two instructors, saying: 'That's a crate of beer, then.' Naval officers have been trained in Dartmouth since 1863 when the old wooden wall HMS Britannia was first moored on the River Dart. The college opened on its current site, high on a hill above Dartmouth, in 1905: the foundation stone was laid by King Edward VII in 1902 and the first cadets entered the college three years later.

TIVERTON

St Peter's Church, St Peter's Street, Tiverton, Devon EX16 6RP

Top: William at Britannia Royal Naval College, Dartmouth. Above: St Peter's Church.

This Grade I listed parish church has two distinctions: it was the location of Samuel Reay's first organ performance of Mendelssohn's 'Wedding March' (at the society wedding of Dorothy Carew and Tom Daniel in 1847) and was the venue for the 2010 wedding of Prince George's godmother Emilia d'Erlanger to old Etonian David Jardine-Paterson. William and Kate caused quite a commotion in the market town when they attended the wedding in the 15th century church, described by art historian Nikolaus Pevsner as a 'gorgeously ostentatious display of civic pride'. Emilia, an interior designer, has known William since he was a teenager (she went on a cruise with the 17-year-old which was nicknamed the 'love boat' cruise as he invited so many girls) and was at school with Kate. She is credited with introducing the royal couple. Her husband David, a renewable energy consultant, is a scion of Scottish landowners – he wore tartan trousers to his wedding – and is descended from the illustrious Hong Kong bankers Jardines.

DORSET

BOVINGTON

Bovington Garrison, Bovington, Wareham, Dorset BH20 6JB

The garrison town in the depths of Dorset has bitter sweet memories for William and Kate. The prince was stationed at the British Army barracks for a ten-week tank commander course in 2007 after joining the Blues & Royals but he lived up to the regiment's reputation – and nickname – as the 'Booze & Royals' leading to a temporary split from his girlfriend. Instead of driving 130 miles up to London to see Kate, he lived the life of a single man with fellow officers from the Household Cavalry, painting the nearby town of Bournemouth red and flirting with girls, who sold their stories to the tabloids. However the couple was back together by the time of William's raucous graduation ball, which was entitled 'Freakin' Naughty' and he only had eyes for her in the officers' mess, which was packed with soldiers and their guests dressed as naughty nuns, doctors and nurses. The Armour Centre is the British Army's training centre of excellence in the core skills of armed warfare: driving and maintaining armoured fighting vehicles (AFVs), operating vehicle weapons' systems and communications equipment. Recruits are trained at its 10,000 acre site, on a fleet of 180 AFVs , using an eight-kilometre all-weather driving circuit, 75km cross-country driving circuit and extensive firing ranges.

PORTLAND

Weymouth and Portland National Sailing Academy, Osprey Quay, Portland, Dorset DT5 1SA

The Duchess of Cambridge is a keen sailor – during her gap year she crewed a yacht around the Solent – so she looked very much at home when she visited the National Sailing Academy during the 2012 Olympics. After flying from Kensington Palace to Weymouth, she joined Princess Anne, her husband Sir Timothy Laurence and Olympic champion Sir Steve Redgrave, who has won five gold medals, on a boat to watch the women's Laser Radial medal race. Back on dry land, she met British competitors and joked with Ben Ainslie, who showed her his latest gold medal which made him the most decorated Olympic sailor of all time. He has won medals at five consecutive Olympic Games. The National Sailing Academy was formally opened by the Princess Royal in 2005 on the site of the former Royal Naval Air Station at Portland which closed at the turn of the Millennium.

Top: William in training at Bovington.
Left: Kate shares a joke with Sir Ben
Ainslie at the National Sailing Academy.

GLOUCESTERSHIRE

CHELTENHAM

Cheltenham Racecourse, Prestbury Park, Cheltenham, Gloucestershire GL50 4SH

Above: race goers pack the stands at Cheltenham Racecourse.

The National Hunt Festival, one of the highlights of the racing calendar, was a favourite of the Queen Mother, who rarely missed the occasion, attending latterly in a buggy painted in her racing colours. The younger generation of royals has followed in her footsteps. In fact the racecourse has been the setting of some of the Duke and Duchess of Cambridge's most memorable scenes: the 2006 Cheltenham Gold Cup where Kate appeared in the royal box for the first time with Prince Charles and the Duchess of Cornwall without William; the opening day of the National Hunt Festival, the following year, when a strained-looking William and Kate made their last public appearance together before their temporary split and at Cheltenham, in 2013, when a pregnant Kate giggled as friend Harry Aubrey-Fletcher dared to tweak Prince William's ear. The Cheltenham Gold Cup, a three-mile flat race, has been held in Prestbury Park since 1831 after its original grandstand in Cleeve Hill was burnt to the ground. Angry churchgoers had disrupted the previous year's race meeting after their parish priest Reverend Francis Close preached on the evils of horseracing and organisers felt that it was wise to move the racecourse to a different location.

CHERINGTON

St Nicholas' Church, Cherington, Gloucestershire GL8 8SN

Above: the Norman church where Mia Grace Tindall was christened in front of the Queen.

Not many churches can boast that they have hosted a royal christening let alone one attended by the Queen, the Duke of Edinburgh, Princess Anne and Prince William. But this tiny Norman church, which is made of rubble and masonry and seats 130 people, was the venue of the christening of Mia Grace Tindall, 16th in line to the throne. And a 'nervous' vicar baptised her in its 12th century font in front of traces of medieval wall paintings. William's cousin Zara and her former England Rugby captain husband Mike Tindall chose the church because it is five minutes away from Gatcombe Park, Princess Anne's house in Gloucestershire, where Zara grew up with her brother Peter Phillips (his daughter Isla was also christened at the church). The Duchess of Cambridge, who was pregnant, remained at home with baby George.

CIRENCESTER

Cirencester Park Polo Club, The Bothy, Cirencester Park, Cirencester, Gloucestershire GL7 1UR

The royals have had a long history with Cirencester Park Polo Club, which was inaugurated in 1894 by the seventh Earl Bathurst. The Prince of Wales, later Edward VIII was the first member of the royal family to play polo there during the 1920s; the Duke of Edinburgh was a regular at tournaments in the 1960s and Prince Charles played in many charity matches up until his retirement from the sport. It was at Cirencester Park Polo Club that Prince William spent his first Father's Day as a parent and Prince George kicked his first ball in public. The Duchess of Cambridge took the 11-month-old toddler along to watch William and uncle Harry playing in the Jerudong Trophy polo match but he did not want to sit still: the moment Kate put him down he headed into the path of a polo pony. He even grabbed a polo stick in an attempt to join in the fun as well as aiming a kick at a ball with his left foot, suggesting that he might, like his father, grandfather Prince Charles and great-grandmother the Queen, be left-handed.

Above: Kate holds Prince George as she watches William play polo on Father's Day. Right: William and Harry at the Jerudong Trophy polo match.

15

COATES

Tunnel House Inn, Tarlton Road, Coates, Cirencester, Gloucestershire GL7 6PW

Above: William and Harry's local, the Tunnel House Inn.

The Tunnel House Inn, nestled between Coates and Tarlton in the Cotswolds, was one of Prince William and Prince Harry's locals when they were staying with their father at Highgrove. With its long tree-lined drive, roaring fires and friendly ambience, the free house was a regular haunt of the two princes until their close friend Guy Pelly, a former student at Cirencester Agricultural College, was secretly filmed allegedly smoking cannabis there. William, who was on a break from Sandhurst, was having a drink with Kate and his cousins Zara and Peter Philips when the filming occurred. Pelly later claimed he was deliberately set up having been passed what he thought was a cigarette by a pretty girl. Originally built during the 18th century as lodgings for navvies working on the Sapperton canal tunnel – hence the name – the pub was rebuilt after two consecutive fires destroyed the building in 1952, leaving only the sign above the door intact (it was not even scorched).

DOUGHTON

Highgrove House, Doughton, Tetbury, Gloucestershire GL8 8TN

Above: Highgrove House, Prince Charles' private residence, where William and Harry grew up.

Owned by the Duchy of Cornwall, Highgrove House is the country home of Prince Charles. He has lived on the estate since 1980 (a year before his marriage to Princess Diana) and has devoted much energy to transforming its 900-acre grounds. Highgrove is also where Princes William and Harry grew up (they had a den with a bar in the basement dubbed Club H) and which William notoriously 'buzzed' on his first training exercise as a helicopter pilot. A gilt-embossed invitation to Highgrove is highly coveted. Kate received her first in 2007 when she was invited to the Duchess of Cornwall's 60th birthday banquet after she and William got back together. Wearing a long white gown, she looked totally relaxed at the formal black-tie ball as she sipped champagne and cocktails in the gardens of Highgrove with Zara Phillips and Mike Tindall. Harry and his then girlfriend Chelsy Davy were unable to make the party as they were on holiday, but there were plenty of celebrity guests, including the comedians Joan Rivers and Stephen Fry, TV presenter Jools Holland, actors Dame Judi Dench and Edward Fox, actress Joanna Lumley and her conductor husband Stephen Barlow and actor Timothy West, with his wife Prunella Scales. After dinner – a three-course organic meal – Kate and William made their

Above: the Highgrove gardens, which have been lovingly restored by Prince Charles.

way onto the dance floor, where the prince mouthed the lyrics of the Frank Sinatra song It Had To Be You to his girlfriend. She was also invited to Prince Charles' 60th birthday celebration the following year, and mingled with senior members of the royal family including Princess Anne and her husband Commander Tim Laurence, the Duke of York, the Earl and Countess of Wessex, Viscount Linley and Lady Sarah Chatto. This time guests were entertained by singer Rod Stewart, who waved his normal £1 million fee as a birthday present to the future King. Prince Charles has spent his time at Highgrove creating one of Britain's most famous gardens, which is both organic and sustainable: he has built a reed bed sewage system for all waste water, all green waste is recycled for mulching and compost and only natural fertilizers are used. He has also created a wild flower meadow, with more than 30 different native plants, grows rare and endangered fruit and vegetables in the Kitchen Garden and is responsible for looking after the national collection of Beech trees and Hostas. In fact he is so proud of his garden that he welcomes visitors.

EASTLEACH

Macaroni Wood, Eastleach, Cirencester, Gloucestershire GL7 3NF

While Prince William grew up in Gloucestershire, his wife was no stranger to the royal county: when she was nine years old she and younger sister Pippa went on a pack holiday with the 1st Andrew's pack of Brownies, to Macaroni Wood, which is set in an Area of Outstanding Natural Beauty in the Cotswolds. The summer camp was based in an old RAF hospital building in 17 acres of woodland, on the Hatherop Estate. There the two sisters fed chickens, collected eggs, watched chicks hatch, bottle-fed lambs and kid goats, rode horses and went for horse-and-cart rides. There was also a playground with rope swings, a slide, a sandpit, a playhouse and a barbecue. The group slept in sleeping bags on camp bunk beds in two dormitories, cooked, washed up, and made their own beds. After making puppets and Easter chicks, they were given their toymakers' badge. According to local legend the wood was named after 18th century dandies, who used to stay in a wooden building on the estate. It was commissioned at the start of World War II by the MoD, who built a runway for the Parachute Regiment to train on Air Speed Oxfords, which towed gliders, and is now owned by the philanthropic organisation the Ernest Cook Trust, who acquired it from the Bazley family, who had owned the Hatherop Estate for more than 130 years.

Below: Members of the 1st Andrew's pack of Brownies on summer camp in Macaroni Wood. Kate is second left in the back row. Pippa is in the centre of the front row.

Minchinhampton

Gatcombe Park, Minchinhampton, Gloucestershire GL6 9AT

Bought by the Queen for Princess Anne and her first husband Captain Mark Phillips (Anne now lives in the 18th century manor house with her second husband Sir Timothy Laurence), Gatcombe Park is known for hosting the Festival of British Eventing over the first weekend of August. The event attracts some of the world's top Olympians as well as more than 40,000 spectators, drawn to its 730-acre grounds with a lake containing brown trout. Kate was one of those visitors in 2005, shortly after leaving St Andrews University. Her appearance, in the Stetson she had worn on safari in Africa, sparked speculation of an imminent engagement but it would be another five years before William got down on bended knee. Gatcombe's Grade II listed manor house was built in Bath stone for local clothier Edward Sheppard and comprises nine bedrooms, four reception rooms, a library, billiard room and conservatory as well as staff quarters. It was purchased by the Queen in 1976 from former Home Secretary and Master of Trinity College, Cambridge, Lord Butler of Saffron Walden. The Crown paid for its renovation and redecoration.

Northleach

St Peter and St Paul's Church, Market Place, Northleach, Gloucestershire GL54 3EE

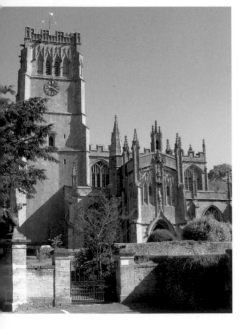

The medieval St Peter and St Paul's Church was put on the map in 2010 when show jumper Harry Meade, an old Etonian friend of William, tied the knot with his wife Rosemarie, a primary school teacher. It was the last wedding that William and Kate attended before they announced their betrothal. In fact they were secretly engaged – William had proposed during a ten-day break in Kenya. The wedding was also memorable because it was attended by three of William's old flames Jecca Craig, Rose Farquhar and Olivia Hunt. Known as the 'Cathedral of the Cotswolds', the present church owes much to the wealth of wool men in Northleach during the 15th century, who bequeathed sums to the church, to fund its nave, aisles, chapels and porch. However its chancel and 100ft tower date from the 13th century and its pitched roof, sacristy door and elaborate stone font, carved with angels playing musical instruments, date from the 14th century.

Above left: eventing at Gatcombe Park. Left:
St Peter and St Paul's Church, known as the
'Cathedral of the Cotswolds'.

WESTONBIRT

Beaufort Polo Club, Down Farm, Westonbirt, Tetbury, Gloucestershire GL8 8QW

There are not many better places to watch Prince William's competitive spirit than at Beaufort Polo Club, which has been the scene of much sibling rivalry with younger brother Harry. Prince

Charles, who is close friends of the club owners Simon and Claire Tomlinson, is patron of the historic club, which the couple revived 19 years ago from one of the first country polo clubs. The Tomlinson boys Luke, a former England polo captain, and his international polo-player brother Mark, have been close friends of the royal princes since they were teenagers. In fact William was an usher at Mark's wedding to Olympic dressage gold medallist Laura Bechtolsheimer. But on the polo field they have been rivals, Harry playing for the Beaufort Polo Club in the annual Goldin Group Charity Cup while William captained the Royal Salute Team – on both occasions William lost to Harry. Kate was first spotted at the club on William's 26th birthday in 2008 with Harry's ex-girlfriend Chelsy Davy watching England – captained by Luke – beat New Zealand in the Williams de Broë International Test Match. The original Beaufort Polo Club was inaugurated in 1872 by Colonel Frank Henry, who had just returned from the ninth Lancers, the regiment which brought the sport to England. It is named after the Duke of Beaufort, who was President in 1928.

Left: William captains the Royal Salute team.

SOMERSET

BISHOPS LYDEARD

St Mary's Church, Church St, Bishops Lydeard, Taunton, Somerset TA4 3AT

When the Duchess's old schoolfriend Alice St John Webster married Gerald Avenel at the Grade I listed St Mary's Church in 2012 it was a reunion of the royal exes: guests included William's former girlfriends Rose Farquhar and Olivia Hunt and Kate's love interests Willem Marx and Henry Ropner. Rose, an aspiring actress, dated William after he left Eton while Olivia went out with him briefly at university. Willem Marx, a journalist, was Kate's first boyfriend while Henry was seen with her when she and William broke up. The 14th and 15th century St Mary's Church is widely believed to be one of the finest historic churches in Somerset with its tall rose-tinted 14th century perpendicular tower, which is built from sandstone from the Quantock Hills. Its interior is equally stunning with a 16th century rood screen, Jacobean pulpit, intricate pew carvings and the royal charter of Edward I.

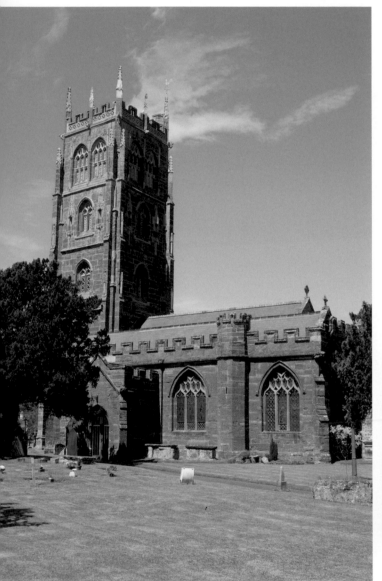

Left: the distinctive perpendicular tower of St Mary's Church. Above: the intricate carvings of the pews.

WILTSHIRE

EAST KNOYLE

Clouds House, East Knoyle, Salisbury, Wiltshire SP3 6BE

Until 2012, the drug and alcohol dependence treatment centre Clouds House was better known as the place where former Take That singer Robbie Williams spent six weeks in rehab. But now the Duchess of Cambridge has upped the profile of 'Clouds', which is run by Action on Addiction, by making a secret visit there on the day her husband arrived in the Falklands in 2012. She later announced that she would be patron of Action on Addiction, following in the footsteps of Princess Diana, who was patron of Turning Point. The Grade II* listed building also has an architectural heritage: designed by Arts and Crafts architect Philip Webb for Conservative politician Percy Wyndham and his wife Madeline, it was frequented by artists such as Edward Burne-Jones and politicians such as Arthur Balfour. It was completed in 1886 but had to be rebuilt after it was destroyed by a fire. It has been a treatment centre since 1983 and has been run by Action on Addiction since 2007.

Below: Clouds House.

LACOCK

St Cyriac's Church, Church Street, Lacock, Wiltshire SN15 2LB

The village of Lacock has both royal and Hollywood connections: it was the setting for the BBC series Pride & Prejudice and Cranford and has long been associated with Prince William's stepmother the Duchess of Cornwall. She moved to the Grade II listed 19th century Rey Mill House with her children Tom and Laura after the breakdown of her marriage to their father Andrew Parker Bowles. Laura and Harry Lopes, an old Etonian, former Calvin Klein model, held their 2006 wedding reception there. Two thousand people lined the streets to catch a glimpse of the couple and their royal guests Prince Charles, Prince William and Prince Harry after the ceremony at St Cyriac's parish church. William arrived by coach with Kate – although the couple had attended a society wedding together, it was the first time that Kate had been invited to a family wedding, showing the extent to which she had been assimilated into the royal family. Lacock became prosperous in the medieval era through the wood and cloth trade as it was located on the London to Bath Road. This prosperity led to the rebuilding of the medieval church in the 15th century to create the Grade I listed perpendicular church on a cruciform plan we see today. Its recessed octagonal tower was added in 1604 and the chancel was remodelled in 1902 by architect Sir Harold Brakspear as a memorial to photographic pioneer William Henry Fox Talbot. The village is also home to the Fox Talbot Museum, which is housed in his former home Lacock Abbey, now owned by the National Trust and rented out to film companies - Harry Potter fans will recognise it as the interior of Hogwarts.

Above: Lacock's medieval St Cyriac's Church, which has both royal and Hollywood connections.

MALMESBURY

Malmesbury Abbey, Gloucester St, Malmesbury, Wiltshire SN16 0AA

Top: the 12th century Malmesbury Abbey.
Above: Malmesbury Abbey's impressive
vaulted ceiling.

Set in the historic city of Malmesbury – thought to be the first capital of England – the stunning Norman church Malmesbury Abbey was the venue for the 2014 wedding of Princes William and Harry's childhood friend Victoria Inskip to Robert Davies-Jones. Both princes attended the wedding in traditional morning dress but the Duchess of Cambridge was unable to attend as she was suffering from hyperemesis gravidarum (or morning sickness). Victoria, who is known as Tor to her friends, and her younger brother Tom, known as Skippy, grew up with the princes and were regulars at their Highgrove Club H. Their father Owen, a field master of the Beaufort Hunt, is a friend of Prince Charles. The service caused amusement among the guests – everyone laughed during the hymn Tell Out, My Soul, when they came to the line 'Proud hearts and stubborn wills are put to flight' as the Prince is known to have a stubborn streak. Malmesbury has been at the cutting edge of royal history since it became home to the first saint of Wessex, Aldheim. The first King of Wessex, Athelstan, who was the grandson of King Alfred, is buried in the Abbey. The present building dates from 1180 and once had a spire taller than Salisbury Cathedral and an impressive tower. But both the spire and tower fell in the 15th and 16th centuries and only the nave, with its breath-taking Norman porch, survives.

MARLBOROUGH

Marlborough College, Bath Rd, Marlborough, Wiltshire SN8 1PA

The Duchess of Cambridge was 14 years old when she arrived at the renowned public school Marlborough College in 1996 – midway through the academic year. It was here, over the next four years of her life, that she blossomed from a shy schoolgirl into the poised young woman, who would marry a prince. She was rumoured to have had a poster of William on the wall above her bed. Nicknamed 'Middlebum', a play on her name, Kate became known for her 'goofy' behaviour – she is even rumoured to have mooned out of the window of her dorm - although she rarely joined in the wilder antics. One schoolmate wrote in the leavers' yearbook for 2000: 'Catherine's perfect looks are renowned but her obsessions with her tits are not. She is often found squinting down her top screaming: "They're growing!" Set in extensive grounds in the quaint market town of Marlborough, the college is one of Britain's finest boarding schools with fees of more than £33,000 a year. The college, which has the motto 'Deus Dat Incrementum' – 'God Giveth the Increase', or 'God Gives Growth' – from 1 Corinthians 3:6, was founded in 1843 for the sons of Church of England clergymen and within a few decades it had become one of the country's leading boys' public schools. Although it now attracts the children of peers and socialites, former pupils (known as old Marlburians) are an eclectic bunch, including Poet Laureate Sir John Betjeman, art historian and Soviet spy Anthony Blunt, round-the-world yachtsman Francis Chichester, actor James Mason, First World War poet Siegfried Sassoon, Conservative politician Rab Butler and singer Chris de Burgh. Built beside the Marlborough Mound, an ancient man-made knoll thought once to have formed part of a Norman motte-and- bailey castle, the college is centred round a courtyard dominated by a Victorian Gothic chapel with stained-glass windows by William Morris. But the school campus, bordered by the River Kennet, is sprawled across the town. Today, the college has its own trout ponds and an observatory as well as extensive playing fields. There are 11 rugby pitches, seven soccer pitches, eight cricket squares, six hockey pitches, three lacrosse pitches, two volleyball courts, 12 tennis courts and a driving range. It was in that sporty atmosphere that Kate thrived. A keen sportswoman, she was in the girls' boarding house Elmhurst, once a 19th century private house. It had its own garden and purpose-built sixth-form wing and was a short walk from the central courtyard. The diligent teenager played hockey for the school, was in the first doubles team at tennis, was a keen netball player and cross-country runner and used to beat the boys at high jump, as she had done before at primary school. She was apparently awarded so many honours at speech day that she barely had a chance to return to her seat between presentations. She was equally academic: she gained three A levels – A grades in mathematics and art and a B in English – meaning that she could go to the university of her choice – and meet her prince.

Above: Marlborough College, where Kate, Pippa and James were pupils.

TIDWORTH

Tedworth House, Tidworth, Wiltshire SP9 7AJ

Above: William and Harry visit Tidworth House.

Help for Heroes has been close to the royal princes' hearts since they became members of the Armed Forces – Harry has served twice in Afghanistan. So they were the natural choice to open Tedworth House, one of the charity's four recovery centres for wounded veterans, serving personnel and their families, on the edge of Salisbury Plain. The two brothers visited the centre in 2013, met wounded personnel and their families and were shown around the state-of-the art adaptive training facilities the Phoenix Centre with its sports hall, swimming pool and gym, and Skiplex, which has an indoor ski simulator. They met wounded personnel and their families at a charity barbecue and Harry was reunited with members of the Warrior Games team, which has won more than 20 medals competing against athletes from the US military. Help for Heroes runs four recovery centres: Tidworth, Colchester, Catterick and Plymouth, which provide sports and physical recovery, educational and training courses, links to other charities and mental wellbeing assistance. The Royal British Legion is contributing £17.5 million towards the cost of running them.

WILTON

St Mary and St Nicholas' Church , West Street, Wilton, Wiltshire SP2 0DL

This 19th century church's claim to fame was hosting the wedding of William's old schoolfriend Tom Sutton and his wife Harriet, who is the niece of a young Princess Diana's boyfriend Dr James Colthurst. William was an usher at the 2011 ceremony, while Kate arrived with friend Louise Aubrey-Fletcher. But it was Pippa who stole the show, turning up with her then boyfriend, former England cricketer turned City banker Alex Loudon, sparking rumours of an engagement. St Mary and St Nicholas was built at the instigation of the Dowager Countess of Pembroke for £20,000 on a north-south axis – as was the custom for churches in her native Russia - and is Romanesque in style. It has marble columns, imported from a 2nd century BC Temple of Venus at Porto Venere, 12th and 13th century stained glass from Florence and a 105ft campanile.

Above: St Mary and St Nicholas' Church.
Left: the church's marble columns date back to the 2nd century BC.

BERKSHIRE

ASCOT

Ascot Racecourse, Ascot, Berkshire SL5 7JX
Coworth Park, Blacknest Rd, Ascot, Berkshire SL5 7SE

Previous page: Osborne House.
Above: Ascot Racecourse.

It was at Ascot racecourse in 2011 – two months after the royal wedding – that Prince William proved he was true to his word and would not let his parents-in-law be side lined. In a first for the royal family, the Queen invited Carole and Michael Middleton to join the royal procession at Ascot's exclusive summer race meeting. The couple joined Fitri Hay, wife of horse owner Jim Hay, in a carriage preceding the Monarch and mingled in the royal box with Princess Anne and Princess Beatrice. Their attendance came 300 years after the venue's first-ever race. Queen Anne, who coincidentally was the daughter of Anne Hyde - the last commoner before Kate to marry into the royal family - spotted the potential of the town for hosting a racecourse. However it was George IV, who, in 1825, started the tradition in which the Queen and her guests arrive at Royal Ascot by horse-drawn landaus, travelling down the straight mile before circling the parade ring. He had commissioned the Royal Enclosure, a two-storey stand built with a surrounding lawn. Ascot is one of the highlights of the social season – gentlemen are required to wear morning dress and top hats in the Royal Enclosure while ladies are expected to wear hats. Visitors who do not have an invitation into the Royal Enclosure, can buy tickets for the Silver Ring, which is located on the straight mile, or the Grandstand.

Ascot is also home to Coworth Park, which has the distinction of being the only hotel in the United Kingdom which has its own polo fields: it is managed by the Guards Polo Club and affiliated to the Hurlingham Polo Association. On top of that, resident coach Andrew Hine is the only polo player in the country to have both captained and managed the England team. Guests of the hotel can make use of its polo facilities and have the bonus of being able to watch Princes William and Harry play polo – they may even spot the Duchess of Cambridge watching her husband from the sidelines. Coworth Park began life in the 18th century as the country mansion Coworth House and has been home to several illustrious families including the 17th Earl of Derby. In the late 19th century the future Edward VII and Queen Alexandra stayed at Coworth House while attending the races at Ascot. Now a 70-room country house hotel and spa, set in 240 acres of parkland, it offers tennis, croquet and horse riding and even has its own helipad – perfect for the royal family.

Above: the luxurious Coworth Park Hotel and spa. Right: William plays polo at Coworth Park.

ASHAMPSTEAD COMMON

Party Pieces, Childs Court Farm, Ashampstead Common, Reading, Berkshire RG8 8QT

Ashampstead Common is the home of the Duchess of Cambridge's family's business Party Pieces, which claims to be 'the UK's leading online and catalogue party company'. Set up by Kate's parents Michael and Carole Middleton, it moved into its current premises, a collection of farm buildings in Ashampstead Common, in 1995. Eight customer service staff now work in the 200-year-old barn, taking orders, while packers work in the picking room, based in a converted cowshed and in the warehouse, a converted hayloft stacked to the roof with themed tableware, decorations, party bags and games. Kate's sister Pippa works for the company and is a part-time editor of its blog, The Party Times, while her brother James sells his cake-making kits through the website. However the company has raised eyebrows over its willingness to exploit royal landmarks such as Kate's wedding to Prince William, the Queen's Diamond Jubilee and the royal tour of Australia. They brought out a Britannia range in 2011 ahead of the royal wedding; a Jubilee range, including canapé flags featuring crown-wearing corgies, in 2012; and a range of 'Australia Day' merchandise, such as flip flop balloons in 2014, sparking accusations they are milking their daughter's profile. Recently they were the subject of a diatribe about 'disappointing service' by TV adventurer Ben Fogle's wife Marina, a former party planner, when the company failed to deliver in time for their son Ludo's fifth birthday. 'Really disappointing service from @PartyPieces [who] failed to deliver for Ludo's party,' she wrote, 'didn't tell me and can "only apologise". Not good enough.' Within half an hour staff had tweeted a grovelling reply and sent a gift in the post. The Party Pieces message read: '@FogleMarina Apologies again, we understand our customer services manager has refunded you and is sending a small gift by way of apology.'

BRADFIELD

St Andrew's Church, Ashampstead Road, Bradfield, Berkshire RG7 6BX

This building, on the banks of the River Pang, was once one of the most famous churches in Britain because of its royal connections. The Duchess of Cambridge, her sister Pippa and brother James, were all christened in the flint-and-chalk building, which had a graceful 14th century north aisle. But now the Grade II* listed building has been sold, causing uproar among its congregation – more than 200 people attended the final service on St Andrew's Day in 2014.

Above: the offices of Party Pieces, the Middleton family firm. Left: St Andrew's Church, Bradfield, where Kate was christened.

BRADFIELD SOUTHEND

**Bradfield Church of England Primary, Cock Lane, Bradfield Southend,
Berkshire RG7 6HR
St Peter's Church, Southend Road, Bradfield Southend, Berkshire RG7 6EU
West View, Cock Lane, Bradfield Southend, Berkshire RG7 6HR**

The neighbouring village of Bradfield Southend is synonymous with Kate's childhood: she lived there for the first 13 years of her life, going to the local toddler group, pre-school and Brownies in St Peter's Church hall (she was in the 1st St Andrew's pack) and attending Bradfield Church of England primary school, next door to her home. Her parents bought West View - opposite the village green and down the road from the Queen's Head pub – for £34,700 in 1979, the year before they got married, and sold it 16 years later for £158,000. Set back from the road, with a large garden, the Victorian house was converted into two semi-detached homes, with bathrooms at the back, during Edwardian times. When the Middletons moved in, it had three bedrooms on the first floor. Keen to improve their investment, Michael, who was good at restoring houses, converted one of the bedrooms into a bathroom, doing the plumbing himself and built another two bedrooms in the loft. Like many other homeowners, the couple also extended the kitchen and built a playroom for the children.

Above left: Kate as a Brownie. Left: Kate as a schoolgirl. Above: Bradfield Church of England Primary School. Above right: West View, the house where Kate grew up.

BUCKLEBURY

The Bladebone Inn, Chapel Row, Bucklebury, Berkshire RG7 6PD
Bucklebury Farm Park, Bucklebury, Berkshire RG7 6RR
Oak Acre, The Avenue, Bucklebury, Berkshire RG7 6NS
Peach's Stores, Long Grove, Upper Bucklebury, Berkshire RG7 6QU

Ten miles from Windsor Castle, Bucklebury is the parish where Kate grew up from the age of 13 until she left home. The quintessential English village, which would not look out of place in the TV series Midsomer Murders, is home to John Madejski, the multi-millionaire owner of Reading Football Club, DJ Chris Tarrant, singer Kate Bush and TV personality Melinda Messenger. Michael and Carole Middleton moved there in 1995 (they bought the five-bedroom, red-brick house Oak Acre, for £250,000) and have lived in the village ever since. They sold their original home, in Chapel Row, in 2012 for £2.3 million and now live in a £4.85 million manor, two miles down the road, which was where Prince George spent the first few months of his life (Carole took him to Bucklebury Farm Park). The Middleton family (and Prince William) are often spotted in the local community, shopping at the local Bladebone Butchery (now the Blackbird Café) and Peach's Stores (William and Kate are fans of Haribo sweets and mint Viennetta ice cream), drinking in the picturesque 17th century Bladebone Inn and attending the traditional August Bank holiday fair. (In fact the Middletons showed their gratitude by inviting butcher Martin Fidler and his wife Sue and shopkeepers Chan and Hash Shingadia to the royal wedding.) The prince first visited the village for Kate's 21st birthday party in 2003. He arrived late and left after the sit-down dinner, which was held in a marquee, but his appearance was significant and showed how close the royal flatmates had become. Five years later, he caused even more of a stir when he landed a £10 million Chinook helicopter in Kate's back garden to practice his take-off and landing skills.

Above right: Kate's parents Carole and Michael Middleton outside their former home in Bucklebury after the couple announced their engagement. Top left: The Bladebone Inn. Middle left: St Mary's Church, the Middleton's local church. Bottom left: Peach's Stores.

BURNHAM

75 Huntercombe Lane North, Burnham, Berkshire SL1 6DX

The Berkshire village of Burnham has attracted a number of celebrities including TV presenter Ulrika Jonsson, comedienne Tracey Ullman and comic Jimmy Carr – who went to Burnham Grammar School. But it was also the home of Kate's maternal grandparents Ronald and Dorothy Goldsmith, who are the parents of Carole Middleton and her younger brother Gary. The couple retired to Burnham after Gary left home.

COLD ASH

Downe House, Hermitage Road Col, Hermitage Road, Cold Ash, Thatcham, Berkshire RG18 9JJ

Downe House is the school that Kate would rather forget: she joined the boarding school as one of a handful of day girls after leaving St Andrew's Pangbourne in 1995 but left midway through the academic year after allegedly being 'a fish out of water'. She later chose the anti-bullying charity Beatbullying as a beneficiary of the Royal Wedding Charitable Gift Fund, in a subtle nod to the fact that she was bullied. Downe House was founded in 1907 - with just three pupils - in Charles Darwin's former home in Downe, Kent, hence the name. It moved to its current location, in 110-acre grounds, in 1922, and has educated thousands of girls including Lady Gabriella Windsor, BBC sports presenter Clare Balding, model Sophie Dahl and comedienne Miranda Hart.

Above: Ronald and Dorothy Goldsmith.
Right: Downe House School.

DORNEY

St James the Less Church, Court Lane, Dorney, Berkshire SL4 6QP

Above: St James the Less Church, the wedding venue of Kate's parents, Carole and Michael Middleton.

This Grade I parish church, in the village of Dorney, on the banks of the River Thames (Dorney means 'island of the bumble bee') was the venue for the 1980 marriage of Kate's parents Michael Middleton and Carole Goldsmith, who arrived at the church in a horse and carriage. Not as grand as St Paul's Cathedral – where Prince Charles married Princess Diana - St James the Less was nonetheless an idyllic venue for the wedding of Prince William's mother-in-law. The church is picturesque and typically English: large parts of the building date from the 12th century, it has a wooden 17th century gallery, is decorated with restored medieval paintings and has a Norman font, with fleur-de-lys carvings. The south porch – or entrance to the church – was built in red brick in 1661 to commemorate the birth of Lady Alice Palmer, daughter of Barbara Villiers, Countess Castlemaine, who was the wife of the 1st Earl of Castlemaine and Lord of Dorney and mistress of Charles II.

ENGLEFIELD

St Mark's Church, off The Street, Englefield, Reading, Berkshire RG7 5EN

It is traditional for members of the royal family to join the Queen at Sandringham on Christmas Day. But in 2012, Prince William and the Duchess of Cambridge turned up for family Eucharist and Christmas carols at the parish church in the village of Englefield. The couple were staying with the Middleton family in nearby Bucklebury, as Kate was in the early stages of pregnancy with Prince George, and were in the congregation with Michael, Carole, Pippa and James. St Mark's, which dates back to 1190 and was restored by Sir George Gilbert Scott in the 19th century, has a long association with the Englefield family, which has its own chapel. Its most famous member Sir Thomas Englefield, a 15th century Speaker of the House of Commons, is buried in an elaborate canopied marble tomb in the church.

Above: William and Kate swapped Sandringham for St Mark's Church when they stayed with the Middletons in nearby Bucklebury.

ETON

Eton College, Eton, Windsor, Berkshire SL4 6DW

William's first day at the public school Eton College is 1995 was a significant departure from royal precedent – his grandfather Prince Philip was a pupil at Gordonstoun and he had sent his three sons, Charles, Andrew and Edward to his alma mater. Tragically his time at Eton was marred by the death of his mother Princess Diana in a car crash in Paris in 1997, when he was

15 years old. But he excelled at sport - he was 'Keeper' (in charge) of the swimming team, took up water polo and captained his house football team - was a school prefect and member of the Eton Society (colloquially known as 'Pop') and left with three good A levels (A in geography, B in history of art and C in biology). He returned to the school in 2006 to play in the Eton Field Game (the sport is a cross between rugby and football). Kate turned up at the ground to watch the match and casually strolled up to embrace him – the pictures of her playfully ruffling his thinning hair went around the globe. Eton was founded in 1440 by Henry VI as the 'King's College of Our Lady of Eton besides Wyndsor' to provide education for 70 'poor' boys. The earliest records of school life date from the 16th century and paint a Spartan picture: scholars rose at 5am, chanted prayers while they dressed and were at their desks by 6am; teaching was in Latin and there was just a single hour of play; lessons ended at 8pm and there were two three-week holidays at Christmas (when scholars remained at Eton) and during the summer. The school flourished under George III, who spent much of his time at Windsor, frequently visiting the school and entertaining boys at Windsor Castle. The renowned 'Fourth of June' speech day, which is marked with a cricket match, procession of boats and picnics on 'Agar's Plough' marks the King's birthday. Following that tradition, Prince William regularly popped up for tea with his grandmother the Queen at Windsor Castle.

Above: William as an Eton schoolboy. Above right: Eton College.

ETON DORNEY

Dorney Lake, off Court Lane, Eton Dorney, Windsor, Berkshire SL4 6QP

Owned by Eton College, the privately-owned Dorney Lake (which is open to the public) was the scene of a gold medal at the Paralympics: the Duchess of Cambridge cheered as Britain's mixed cox fours – Pam Relph, Naomi Riches and cox Lily van den Broecke (known as 'the blondes in a boat') rowed to victory with teammates David Smith and James Roe, beating Germany to the medal. Dorney Lake, a world-class rowing and flat-water canoeing centre, is set in 450-acre parkland near Windsor. The lake hosted the rowing and kayak events during the 2012 Olympic and Paralympic Games and was voted top Olympic venue by an exit poll of spectators.

LAMBOURN

St Michael and All Angels, Parsonage Lane, Lambourn, Berkshire RG17 8PA

This church, set in the heart of racehorse country, was the natural setting for the 2011 wedding of English National Hunt jump-jockey Sam Waley-Cohen – the man branded the 'royal matchmaker' after saving Prince William and Kate's romance – and party organiser Annabel Ballin. The Duchess of Cambridge was a surprise guest, turning up just hours after watching her husband take part in his first Trooping of the Colour. The future Queen drove herself to the wedding with her sister Pippa, wearing the same hat she had worn to Horseguards' Parade earlier in the day. Sam, who came second in the 2011 Grand National, is widely credited with saving the royal romance after he invited William and Kate to a party at his family's 17th century mansion in Oxfordshire in June 2007 – three months after they split. The couple spent the evening deep in conversation, sparking rumours that a reunion was on the cards.

Kate is not the only member of the royal family to have been linked to St Michael and All Angels. The church houses an alabaster medallion of Charles I, one of three created after he was executed in 1649, which is rumoured to have been stored by royal sympathisers at Lambourn Place, the manor house, which once stood near the church, before being purchased by the vicar JH Light in the 19th century.

Left: Kate chats to fellow guests at the wedding of Sam Waley-Cohen and Annabel Ballin.

PANGBOURNE

St Andrew's School, Buckhold, Pangbourne, Berkshire RG8 8QA

The village of Pangbourne has bitter-sweet memories for Kate. It was in Pangbourne that her maternal grandfather Ronald Goldsmith died from a heart attack in 2003 – while Kate was at university - after suffering from the neurological disorder Multiple System Atrophy and it was there that she went to prep school. She was seven years old when she started at St Andrew's School, a co-educational part-boarding school, housed in a Victorian mansion and set in 54-acre grounds, in the hamlet of Buckhold. Nicknamed Squeak after one of the two guinea pigs (the other was called Pip) her time at the school was one of the happiest in her life. A natural athlete, she set the school record in her age group for 1.5 metre high jump (which still stands), played goal defence in netball and won swimming races. She also made her debut on the stage, starring as Eliza Doolittle in a production of My Fair Lady; performing in the school's production of the Tchaikovsky ballet The Nutcracker and appearing in a musical called Rats! - an adaptation of the Robert Browning poem The Pied Piper of Hamelin. In her final year she starred in a Victorian melodrama with an interesting twist – her leading man was called William. In a prophetic scene, William dropped onto one knee and asked Kate's character to marry him. 'Yes,' she replied. 'It's all I've ever longed for. Yes, oh yes, dear William . . . Ah, to think I am loved by such a splendid gentleman.' Later in the play, she proclaims: 'I feel there is someone waiting to take me away into a life that's full, bright and alive.' When a fortune teller reveals that she will meet a good-looking and wealthy man, she asks: 'Will he fall in love with me and marry me? Oh, how my heart flutters!' But, unlike in real life, Kate's character is abandoned with her child at the end of the play, as William turns out not to be such a splendid gentleman after all. St. Andrew's School was founded in 1934 in a Victorian Gothic building with just two staff and eight boys. In 2012 the Duchess of Cambridge returned to the school to open its new Astroturf and played hockey in three-inch heels. She was treated to her favourite school lunch - Scottish roast beef and 'birdseed', a mixture of flapjack and Rice Krispie cake - after staff asked St James' Palace what she would like to eat.

Above: St Andrew's School where Kate spent some of the happiest years of her life.

READING

Royal Berkshire Hospital, Craven Road, Reading, Berkshire RG1 5AN

The Royal Berkshire Hospital has been the scene of Middleton births and deaths as well as visits by the royals: the future Queen of England was born, with a mop of dark hair, at the NHS hospital in 1982, her sister Pippa in 1983 and brother James in 1987; Prince William was admitted there when he was eight years old after being accidentally hit on the side of the forehead by a school friend wielding a golf club; and Kate's maternal grandmother Dorothy died there in 2006 after a four-month battle against lung cancer. The Victorian hospital was opened in 1839 on land donated by the 19th century Prime Minister Henry Addington, 1st Viscount Sidmouth, who was a local resident. King William IV took a keen interest in the building – although he died before it was opened so it was left to his niece, Queen Victoria, who succeeded him, to become its first patron. Another famous patient was former fighter pilot Douglas Bader, who had both his legs amputated at the hospital, after an air crash at Woodley Aerodrome. The current Royal Berkshire NHS Foundation Trust was opened by the Queen and the Duke of Edinburgh in 2006 after a £132 million revamp, described as England's biggest Treasury-funded NHS building scheme. They visited a children's ward and the radiology department as well as being given demonstrations of a robotic arm and angioplasty, which uses balloons to open blocked blood vessels.

SLOUGH

33 Arborfield Close, Slough, Berkshire SL1 2JP

This leasehold flat, in a modern 1970s block in a cul-de-sac in Slough, is where the Duchess of Cambridge's parents Michael and Carole Middleton moved in together. In those days Slough was a sprawling industrial suburb populated with factories - it was the headquarters of Mars and Citroen and home to Dulux paint. The apartment was in a convenient location for the couple, who both worked eight miles away at Heathrow Airport (Michael was a flight dispatcher for British Airways while Carole was an air hostess) but by the time they got married, in 1981, they had moved to the more salubrious village of Bradfield Southend.

STANFORD DINGLEY

Old Boot Inn, Stanford Dingley, Berkshire RG7 6LT

The Old Boot Inn is a regular haunt of the Middleton family (and Prince William) and the landlord received a coveted invitation to the royal wedding. After attending the ceremony John Haley raced back to the rustic pub to host a post-ceremony bash in aid of charity, which included a number of villagers, who had also attended the wedding service in Westminster Abbey. John and his partner Pam Brown were even included in the Royal Wedding edition of the Top Trumps card game.

Top: Carole with Kate at 21 days old. Middle: Carole and Michael's first home.
Bottom: the Old Boot Inn, where William and Kate were regulars.

WINDSOR

Victoria Barracks, Sheet Street, Windsor, Berkshire SL4 1HF
Windsor Castle, Windsor, Berkshire SL4 1NJ

Above: Kate presents medals to members of the Irish Guards.

Kate's first military engagement was at Victoria Barracks, the British army barracks, which lies a quarter of a mile south of Windsor Castle. She and Prince William, who is Colonel of the Irish Guards, presented medals to members of the regiment in 2011 after their six-month tour of duty of Afghanistan. The couple also presented the Elizabeth Cross (a medal to recognise the families of those killed in action) to the widows of three soldiers - Major Matthew Collins (Lucy Collins), Lance Sergeant Mark Burgan (Leanne Burgan) and Guardsman Christopher Davies (Emma Johnson). Although they are based in Mons Barracks, in Aldershot, the Irish Guards are involved in public and ceremonial duties at Buckingham Palace, St James' Palace, The Tower of London and Windsor Castle. The Victoria Barracks is home to the Foot Guards, from the Household Division. Accompanied by a regimental band, corps of drums or pipe band, and wearing their full-dress uniform of red tunics and bearskins, they march from the Barracks to the Castle for the 45-minute changing of the guard ceremony, which usually takes place in the Castle's quadrangle at 11am (when the Queen is in residence it takes place on the castle forecourt). Visitors must buy a castle ticket to watch the ceremony.

The oldest and largest occupied castle in the world, Windsor Castle has been the family home of British kings and queens for almost a century. The royal standard flies from the Round Tower when the Queen is in residence: she spends most of her private weekends at Windsor (when William was at Eton he would have tea with her at 4pm on Sunday afternoons), takes up official residence for a month over Easter, known as Easter Court, and spends a week at Windsor each June when she attends Royal Ascot and the service of the Order of the Garter (Prince William became a Knight of the Garter in 2008 in front of a giggling Kate and Harry). Built by William the Conqueror in 1086, high above the river Thames and on the edge of a Saxon hunting ground (a day's march from the Tower of London), Windsor Castle has witnessed all manner of historic occasions: Edward III, who was born at Windsor, created the St George's Hall for gatherings of his newly-founded Order of the Garter; Charles I was imprisoned there before his trial and execution and is buried in St George's Chapel; Prince Albert died of typhoid at Windsor; the Queen and Princess Margaret were evacuated to Windsor during World War II; the Queen and the Duke of Edinburgh celebrated their Golden Wedding anniversary in the newly-restored building, after a fire had raged through the castle, and the Queen hosted a Diamond Jubilee lunch at Windsor with the largest gathering of crowned heads of state since her Coronation. But all of the events were overshadowed by William's 21st birthday party, for which the castle was transformed into an African jungle, with two giant model elephants towering over guests, their trunks intertwined to form an archway to the dance floor - animal skins decorated the walls, a giant giraffe's head took pride of place over the long golden bar, which snaked the length of the room, and a tribal mask stood out from the opposite wall. Three hundred guests, all in fancy dress, danced to the sounds of the band Shakarimba, a six-piece group from Botswana, and William jumped on

Above: the distinctive towers of Windsor Castle, the oldest and largest occupied castle in the world.

stage and played the drums. The Monarch arrived as the Queen of Swaziland, in a white gown, tribal headdress and giant fur wrap, while Prince Charles wore a safari suit and hunting hat, Earl Spencer and Prince Andrew were both dressed as big-game hunters in safari outfits and Princesses Beatrice and Eugenie dressed in matching leopard-skin costumes. The St Andrews set arrived in a battered white van decorated with balloons and tinsel. But Kate's attendance was dwarfed by two events: the first was the arrest of intruder Aaron Barschak, a self-styled 'comedy terrorist', who, despite being dressed as Osama bin Laden, managed to gatecrash the party and stumble onto the stage in the Great Hall, grabbing the microphone from the prince, who was thanking the Queen and Prince Charles for his party; the second was the attendance of Jessica 'Jecca' Craig, the daughter of a wealthy conservationist, who was William's first serious girlfriend (the couple had got close when he visited her family's 45,000- acre wildlife reserve in Kenya during his gap year and there were rumours of a 'pretend engagement'). In order to quash the rumours, William took the unusual step of releasing a public statement denying that he had a girlfriend at all. Within the precincts of the castle lies the 15th century St George's Chapel, spiritual home of the Order of the Garter, the oldest order of chivalry in the world, which was founded by Edward III in 1348 and is the last-remaining honour to be given at the discretion of the sovereign. Begun by Edward IV and completed by Henry VIII, the chapel is one of the finest examples of late medieval architecture in Western Europe. Over the centuries it has witnessed royal christenings, confirmations, weddings and funerals: Harry's 1984 baptism; William's 1997 confirmation; the weddings of Prince Edward and the Duchess of Wessex, in 1999, and Peter and Autumn Phillips, in 2008 (Kate attended alone as William was in Africa) and the 2002 funeral of Princess Margaret. Ten British monarchs lie buried in the chapel - Edward IV, Henry VI, Henry VIII, Charles I, George III, George IV, William IV, Edward VII, George V and George VI – as well as the Queen Mother. But William and Kate's Britain is not just confined to the castle grounds: they have also attended events on Long Walk, which runs 2.65 miles from its George IV gateway to Snow Hill, where there is a Copper Horse statue of King George III, and at the town's Victoria Barracks. Prince William joined the Queen and the Duke of Edinburgh at the Albert and King's Road junction roundabout in 2014 for the unveiling of a statue of the Queen's Windsor Grey horses Daniel & Storm. William was patron of the Windsor Greys Jubilee Appeal to create two life-size sculptures of the lead carriage horses used in state occasions (sculptor Robert Rattray's designs were turned into prints for fundraising).

Above: St George's Chapel in the snow.

WOKINGHAM

Ludgrove School, Wokingham, Berkshire RG40 3AB

William was eight years old when he went to boarding school for the first time. But instead of going to Prince Charles' alma mater Cheam, he was sent to Ludgrove prep school, where alumni included the Duke of Kent and the Duchess of York's father Major Ronald Ferguson. William arrived at the school sandwiched between his parents in the back of a Bentley, shook hands with the headmaster Gerald Barber (he and his wife Janet, who retired in 2008 after 35 years, were invited to the royal wedding) and was shown to his dorm. Within half an hour Diana had returned to London in her Jaguar while Charles, who was walking with a cane after bone-graft surgery, limped back to the Bentley to go back to Highgrove, where he was recuperating. Although he was watched over by bodyguards, William was treated exactly the same as the other 186 students, getting up at 7.15am, washing in the communal bathroom, and beginning classes after prayers and breakfast. Phone calls home were forbidden and he was allowed just three exeat weekends a term. It was at Ludgrove, which was founded in 1892, that William and Harry met the van Straubenzee brothers Thomas and Henry (and younger brother Charlie), who were the nephews of Princess Diana's childhood friend Willie. Thomas, who is married to the Duke of Northumberland's daughter Lady Melissa Percy, accompanied William on his first foreign tour of New Zealand. Henry, who was working as a junior master during his gap year, was killed in a car crash outside the school. The royal princes are joint patrons of the Henry van Straubenzee Memorial Fund.

YATTENDON

The Estate Office, Barn Close, Yattendon, Berkshire RG18 0UY

Yattendon was the first home of the Duchess of Cambridge's family business Party Pieces. Carole Middleton began making party bags at her kitchen table just after the birth of Kate's younger brother James in 1987 and rented a small unit four miles from their home in Bradfield Southend to store her merchandise. She aimed to 'inspire other mothers to create magical parties at home and to make party organising a little easier'. Eight years later the company moved to its current home in Ashampstead Common.

Above: William starts at Ludgrove prep school. Right: Yattendon, the first home of Party Pieces.

BUCKINGHAMSHIRE
MILTON KEYNES

Bletchley Park, Sherwood Drive, Bletchley, Milton Keynes, Buckinghamshire MK3 6EB

Above: Kate at Bletchley Park.

The Duchess of Cambridge's paternal grandmother Valerie Glassborow – and her twin sister Mary – were among 9,000 people who worked at the top-secret Government Code and Cypher School, which broke the Nazi's Engima Code, during World War II. They were working in Hut 16 (as the newly-restored Hut 6 has been renamed) on VJ Day, 15 August 1945, when a message was intercepted from Tokyo to Geneva, indicating that surrender was imminent. Kate was aware that her grandmother – and her twin – worked as Foreign Office civilians in the Cover Management Y section, intercepting enemy signals for decryption. But she was unaware that her grandmother knew about the end of the war – until she unveiled Bletchley Park's £8 million restoration in 2014. There she met a contemporary of her grandmother, Lady Marion Brody, who told her: 'On August 15, 1945, Valerie, Mary and I and two other girls were on the day shift, which was rather fortunate. Mr Williams (an officer) came in. He was smiling. He said: "Well done girls. A signal's been intercepted going from Tokyo to Geneva; the Japanese are about to surrender." We just sat there, shocked into absolute silence. He shuffled from one foot to the other – he didn't know what to do either – then he said: "Well, bloody well get on with your work!" He told us a message had gone to the King and the Prime Minister. It couldn't be announced before the message had gone on from Geneva to London because they would have known we'd been listening. It was a great moment, one that I've remembered all my life.' Valerie and Mary Glassborow went on to marry the Middleton brothers, Peter and Anthony and never talked about their experiences. But visitors to Bletchley Park can now visit the hut where they both worked. It was in August 1938 that a team of M16, members of the Government Code and Cypher School and scholars-turned-codebreakers arrived at the mansion house, set in the Buckinghamshire countryside. Under the guise of 'Captain Ridley's Shooting Party', they looked as if they were friends enjoying a relaxed weekend together – they even bought a chef from the Savoy Hotel to cook their food. But their mission was to scout for a location for the security services to work on cracking the Nazi codes and ciphers (the most important was Enigma). They returned when war broke out in 1939 and set up large pre-fabricated wooden huts on the lawns of the park. Their first break came on January 23, 1940, when a team, working under Dilly Knox, with the mathematicians John Jeffreys, Peter Twinn and Alan Turing (played by Benedict Cumberbatch in the film The Imitation Game), unravelled the Germany Army administration key, known as the 'Green'. They went on to crack the 'Red' key, used by Luftwaffe liaison officers to co-ordinate air support for army units and crack the Enigma code. Thousands of wireless operators tracked the enemy radio nets up and down the dial, logging every letter or figure. The messages were then sent back to Station X (Bletchley Park) where they were deciphered, translated and fitted together like a gigantic jigsaw puzzle by civilians such as Kate's grandmother.

SAUNDERTON

Child Bereavement UK, Clare Charity Centre, Wycombe Road, Saunderton, Buckinghamshire HP14 4BF

The charity Child Bereavement UK has a special resonance with Prince William as he lost his mother as a child. Founding patron Julia Samuel was a close friend of Princess Diana, who made an unscheduled visit to the charity's launch in 1994, despite having retired from public life. A counsellor at St Mary's Hospital, in Paddington, she is one of Prince George's seven godparents. William, who is royal patron of the charity, followed in his mother's footsteps when he toured their headquarters in 2013 with Kate, who was five and a half months pregnant. The couple met staff, bereaved families and fundraisers such as cookery writer Mary Berry, who is a long-term patron of the organisation. The presenter of The Great British Bake Off has raised money for the charity since the death of her 19-year-old son William in 1989. William told her: 'My wife is a big fan of yours - and my tummy is a big fan.' The Child Bereavement Charity supports families who have lost - or are facing the loss - of a child. They train 5, 000 professionals each year (police, nurses and counsellors) on how to deal with families coping with personal loss.

Above: the royal couple tour the headquarters of Child Bereavement UK. Left: the charity's royal patron Prince William and his pregnant wife.

HAMPSHIRE

ALDERSHOT

Mons Barracks, Prince's Avenue, Aldershot, Hampshire GU11 2LF

One of the regular fixtures in the Duke and Duchess of Cambridge's diary is the St Patrick's Day Parade at Mons Barracks. Following in a royal family tradition, Kate's first solo military engagement on March 17, 2012, was presenting shamrocks to 40 officers and guardsmen in

the 1st Battalion Irish Guards at the barracks after their 450-strong parade. Kate, who was wearing a gold Cartier shamrock brooch, which originally belonged to the Queen Mother, even carried a sprig for the regimental mascot, Conmeal - an Irish wolfhound, who had been washed and blow-dried specially for the occasion. Prince William, who is Colonel of the Regiment, accompanied Kate the following year, when she was five-and-a-half months pregnant and famously got her heel stuck in a drain – she grabbed her husband's arm and pulled herself free – and in 2014 when they returned from their five-star holiday in the Maldives. Formed on April 1, 1900, by order of Queen Victoria, in recognition of their courage in the Second Boer War, the Irish Guards are a Foot Guards regiment, based at Mons Barracks but involved in public and ceremonial duties at Buckingham Palace, Windsor Castle, St James' Palace and The Tower of London. The regiment takes its motto 'Quis Separabit' – 'Who shall separate us?' – from the Order of St Patrick, an order of chivalry founded by George III.

Left: resplendent in green, Kate presents shamrocks to officers and guardsman of the 1st Battalion Irish Guards.

GOSPORT

The Royal Navy Submarine Museum, Haslar Jetty Road, Gosport, Hampshire PO12 2AS

As Commodore-in-Chief Submarines and patron of the £7 million HMS Alliance Conservation Appeal, Prince William was the natural choice to attend the 2014 service of re-dedication to the newly-restored submarine - the centrepiece of the Royal Navy's Submarine Museum and its official memorial to submariners. He toured the submarine, met veterans, presented schoolgirl Alegria Tracey with a poetry prize and was given a 'Dolphins' submariner badge with a traditional tot of rum. Designed during World War II and launched in 1945, HMS Alliance was one of 14 'A' class submarines that served in the Far East during the Cold War. She was retired from service after 28 years but began to corrode after she was moored by the museum quayside. Visitors to the museum can now take a 40-minute tour of the submarine's control room, engine room, forward torpedo compartment, galley, heads and accommodation. The museum is also home to The Royal Navy's first submarine Holland 1 and the only surviving WW2 midget submarine X24.

Above: William enjoys a tipple of rum aboard the newly-restored submarine, HMS Alliance.

HOOK

RAF Odiham, Hook, Hampshire RG29 1QT

Codenamed 'Golden Kestrel', William arrived at RAF Odiham in 2008 for the final week of a four-month attachment to its Central Flying School to train with 7 Squadron. The base, which works with Joint Helicopter Command, deploys helicopters worldwide for the Royal Navy, Army and Royal Air Force and operates three Chinook squadrons and one Army Air Corps Lynx squadron. But William's stint, learning to fly a £10million twin-rotor Chinook helicopter, was mired in controversy after he took five 'joyrides' at a cost of £86,434 to the taxpayer. Although he was accompanied by a senior instructor and experienced crew, the flights led to gripes that he was using one of the MoD's 48-strong fleet of Chinooks as his own personal taxi service when the RAF was overstretched in Afghanistan. Having drawn up the flight plans himself, William decided that his first training exercise, on April 2, should be a trip to his family home, Highgrove, where he could 'buzz' his father (it is not known whether Prince Charles was at home at the time). He flew the 106-mile round trip to Gloucestershire. The MoD later claimed that the £11,985 trip was part of a 'general handling exercise'. The following day William practised his take-off and landing skills at Kate's home in Bucklebury. After getting permission from the police and the Middleton family, he flew the 12 miles from his base and circled over the house at 300ft, before landing in a paddock in their grounds. He did not get out of the helicopter but took off 20 seconds later. The trip cost £8,716, but was defended on the grounds that 'battlefield helicopter crews routinely practise landing in fields and confined spaces away from their airfields as a vital part of their training for operations'. However, on April 4, William bent the rules even further, travelling 260 miles to Hexham, Northumberland. While another pilot flew back to base, he travelled on to the Scottish border town of Kelso, to join Kate at the wedding of their close friend Lady Iona Douglas-Home (granddaughter of Sir Alec Douglas-Home and daughter of the chairman of Coutts, who had met the couple at St Andrews) and banker Thomas Hewitt. The most expensive of William's jaunts, at £18,522, the 'general training' flight took 4 hours and 15 minutes but was defended by the MoD as 'a legitimate training sortie'. After returning to base from the wedding, William had to conduct low-level flying training. Having buzzed his father and girlfriend, the obvious choice was his grandmother. He made the 256-mile round trip to the Sandringham estate in Norfolk on April 9, at a cost of £4,358, although the Queen was not there at the time. His final sortie was on April 12 – the day after his graduation ceremony, when he used another Chinook training exercise as an excuse to ferry him and Harry to the Isle of Wight for Peter Phillips' stag do. The official reason given for the £8,716, 190-mile trip was 'open-water training' - the MoD said that the flight was intended to train William in low-level flying, negotiating busy air traffic over London, crossing water, flying in low cloud and landing at an enclosed helipad, but by the time he took the flight William had already been given his wings, and documents revealed under the Freedom of Information Act showed that he had kept his superiors in the dark over the reason for his trip. Air Chief Marshal Sir Glenn Torpy, head of the RAF, was reported to have been furious about the situation and the 'sheer stupidity' of allowing William to make the Isle of Wight flight, asking for a detailed explanation of how it had come about. Even so, the MoD decided that although 'a degree of naivety' had been involved, there should be no punishments as no rules had been broken.

Above: Chinook helicopters in flight.

SOUTHAMPTON

Ocean Terminal, Atlantic Way, Eastern Docks, Southampton, Hampshire SO14 3QN

Above: Kate names the third Royal Princess, the flagship of Princess Cruises.

Ocean Terminal was the venue for the Duchess of Cambridge's last solo engagement before she went on maternity leave in 2013. Twenty-nine years after Princess Diana named the original Royal Princess cruise liner, the Duchess of Cambridge smashed a £1,250 Nebuchadnezzar of Moet & Chandon champagne on its replacement's bow. Built by Fincantieri at their shipyard in Monfalcone, Italy, the 3,600-passenger ship MS Royal Princess (the third to bear its name) is the flagship of the fleet of liners operated by Princess Cruises. Her maiden voyage was four days after the blessing ceremony, which included a performance by the Royal Marines and the pipers of the Irish Guards.

SUTTON SCOTNEY

Naomi House Children's Hospice, Stockbridge Road, Sutton Scotney, Winchester, Hampshire SO21 3JE

The Duchess of Cambridge chose the date of her 2nd wedding anniversary – April 29, 2013 – for her visit to Naomi House to celebrate Children's Hospice Week. While William was on duty as a search and rescue pilot in Anglesey, Kate toured the hospice and met staff, volunteers, supporters, children and their families. And in a nod to her anniversary, she was presented with a framed picture from the children's book the Very Hungry Caterpillar, featuring the children's fingerprints and made in cotton – a traditional symbol for a second wedding anniversary. Naomi House, which was opened in 1997 by Prince Charles, and its sister hospice Jacksplace (which cares for children over 16) support families from seven counties in the South of England – Hampshire, Berkshire, Wiltshire, Dorset, Surrey, West Sussex and the Isle of Wight – and offer palliative care, respite, emergency and end of life care. Their £4 million Caterpillar Appeal aims to update the hospice for the 21st century.

Above and right: Kate visits Naomi House on her 2nd wedding anniversary to celebrate Children's Hospice Week.

ISLE OF WIGHT

BEMBRIDGE

Bembridge Airport, Sandown Road, Bembridge, Isle of Wight PO35 5PW

Managed by the Vectis Gliding Club, Bembridge Airport, which has one concrete runway and one grass strip, was the scene of William's controversial helicopter flight to the Isle of Wight: he caused a furore when, in order to avoid the Friday afternoon rush-hour, he picked up Prince Harry at Woolwich Barracks and flew to the island for Peter Phillips' stag do. The 24-man party, which included Zara Phillips' husband Mike Tindall, stayed in the nearby sailing resort of Cowes.

COWES

The Anchor Inn, 1-3 High Street, Cowes, Isle of Wight PO31 7SA

This 18th century pub was the venue for the start of Peter Phillips' stag do – before his wedding to Autumn Kelly. Prince William joined the group as they spent two days touring the restaurants and bars in Cowes, starting in a restrained fashion in The Anchor Inn and getting wilder as the weekend went on. The Anchor Inn was built in 1704 and originally named the 'House of the Three Trumpeters' – it changed to a more nautical name during the 1820s.

The Anchor Inn, which hosted the royal stag party.

EAST COWES

Osborne House, York Avenue, East Cowes, Isle of Wight PO32 6JX

Prince William's great-great-great-great grandmother Queen Victoria loved this seaside palace where she lived with her husband Prince Albert and their nine children – her first words on visiting were: 'It is impossible to imagine a prettier spot.' Visitors to Osborne House can tour the Royal Apartments, admire the views from the terraces across the Solent (said to remind Prince Albert of the bay of Naples), explore the extensive grounds and stroll along Queen Victoria's private beach, now open to the public for the first time .

Above and left: Queen Victoria's seaside palace Osborne House.

WROTHAM

Wide Horizons, Margaret McMillan House, Gravesend Road, Wrotham, Kent TN15 7JN

When George V's widow Queen Mary visited Margaret McMillan House in 1937 after she came out of mourning – a year after it was opened by her son, the future George VI – she presented them with a tea service and a rocking horse, which had belonged to her daughter Princess Elizabeth. But, 75 years later, the Duchess of Cambridge's visit proved less genteel: she joined a group of inner city children on a camping trip, exploring the woods, building a shelter, chatting around a bonfire and sampling their smoky bread, cooked on the flames. Her visit to the 26-acre site was organised by the charities Wide Horizons and ARK, which are supported by the Foundation of Prince William, Prince Harry and the Duchess of Cambridge, and work with disadvantaged city children. Wide Horizons, which owns Margaret McMillan House, offers 34,000 children a year, who would not otherwise have the opportunity to experience the 'great outdoors', the chance to visit one of their eight day or residential centres.

Right: Margaret McMillan House.

OXFORDSHIRE

BLEDINGTON

The King's Head Inn, The Green, Bledington, Oxfordshire OX7 6XQ

Above right: the pond at The King's Head Inn in Bledington. Top: breakfast for two at The King's Head Inn. Above: the bedroom where William and Kate stayed.

This stunning 16th century Inn, which has two AA Rosettes and is mentioned in the Good Food Guide, gained the royal seal of approval in 2005 after the wedding of Prince William's close friend Hugh van Cutsem to landowner's daughter Rose Astor. It was the first society event that William and Kate attended together just weeks before they graduated from St Andrews University and showed how far their relationship had blossomed. The couple stayed in room 10 - William arrived the night before the wedding for the traditional ushers' breakfast and Kate checked in the following day before the marriage ceremony. They have returned to the pub twice since then – once to dine with Hugh and Rose just weeks before William and Kate's 2007 break-up and once for a buffet after a pub cricket match (William donned his whites to play for Hugh's team against landlord Archie Orr-Ewing). Originally built as a cider house, the King's Head was put on the map when, according to local legend, Prince Rupert of the Rhine, commander of the King's Forces, stayed there during the English Civil War before fighting in the Battle of Stow.

BURFORD

St John the Baptist's Church, Church Green, Burford, Oxfordshire OX18 4RY

Described by Simon Jenkins in his England's Thousand Best Churches as 'the Queen of Oxfordshire', St John the Baptist's Church was the venue for the 2005 wedding of Prince Charles' godson Hugh van Cutsem and landowners' daughter Rose Astor. The occasion was the first society event that the Duke and Duchess of Cambridge attended together just weeks before they graduated from St Andrews University. Kate strolled into the church alone while William, who was an usher, showed guests, including his former girlfriend Jecca Craig, to their seats. Built between 1160 and 1475, the Cotswold 'wool church' houses memorial tablets to Henry VIII's barber-surgeon Edmund Harman and Burford mason Christopher Kempster, who was employed by architect Sir Christopher Wren on the rebuilding of St Paul's Cathedral. A group of Levellers – mutineers from Churchill's army – were imprisoned in the church in 1649 (one of them carved his name on the font) before being forced onto the roof to watch their ringleaders being executed in the churchyard (there is a plaque close to the porch commemorating those executed).

Above: Burford's St John the Baptist's Church boasts stained glass and ornate arches.

CARTERTON

RAF Brize Norton, Carterton, Oxfordshire OX18 3LX

When Prince William returned from the Falklands in 2012, the Duchess of Cambridge was the first to greet him. She drove herself to RAF Brize Norton to meet the prince as he touched down at 4am. RAF Brize Norton, which employs 5,800 service personnel, 1,200 contractors and 300 civilians, is the largest station in the Royal Air Force. It is home to the RAF's Strategic and Tactical Air Transport and Air-to-Air Refuelling. Members of the public can visit – each request is considered on a case-by-case basis.

EWELME

St Mary the Virgin's Church, Ewelme, Parson's Lane, Ewelme, Oxfordshire OX10 6HS

The Church of St Mary the Virgin witnessed one of the Duchess of Cambridge's 'Marilyn' moments – reminiscent of the actress in the film The Seven Year Itch - when a gust of wind caught her black and cream polka dot dress. Kate, who was seven months pregnant, was walking into the 2013 wedding of William's old friend William van Cutsem and City headhunter Rosie Ruck Keene, who is a passionate equestrian, on her own (her husband was an usher) when her skirt flew up revealing her legs. The 15th century parish church, which has a cloister of 13 red brick almshouses, has a distinguished history: it houses the tomb of Geoffrey Chaucer's granddaughter Alice de la Pole, who was the Duchess of Suffolk and founder of the trust 'God's House at Ewelme'. Author Jerome K Jerome, who wrote Three Men in a Boat, and lived in the village in the 1880s, is also buried in the churchyard.

NETTLEBED

St Bartholomew's Church, High Street, Nettlebed, Oxfordshire RG9 5DA

In order to avoid upstaging the bride, the Duchess of Cambridge deliberately stayed out of the limelight during the wedding of Thierry Kelaart and Patrick Heathcote-Amory at the 19th century St Bartholomew's Church. But her family were guests of honour and her father played a central role in the 2012 ceremony, giving away the bride. Thierry, a jeweller, who was at Edinburgh University with Pippa, asked Michael to step in for her late father. Prince William did not attend the ceremony. Instead Kate watched the service with her mother Carole and sister Pippa, before making their way through a side door to the reception at the Kelaart family's farmhouse next door. St Bartholomew's, which has stained glass windows by the renowned artist John Piper was rebuilt in 1846 although parts of its tower date back to Norman times.

Top: Charles, William and Harry leave Brize Norton. Middle: St Mary the Virgin's Church. Bottom: St Bartholomew's Church.

OXFORD

Oxford Spires Academy, Glanville Road, Oxford OX4 2AU
Rose Hill Primary School, The Oval, Oxford OX4 4SF

When the Duke and Duchess of Cambridge got their cocker spaniel puppy, they refused to disclose its name, claiming it was a 'private matter' and they did not want to be accused of 'breaching their own privacy'. But the secret was coaxed out of Kate by Abubakr Hussain, a seven-year-old pupil at Rose Hill Primary School. When he asked Kate what she was going to call the cuddly toy she had been given (pupils are given soft toys in art class), she revealed that she would name the dog Lupo (wolf in Italian) after her own pet. Kate's 2012 trip to Oxford was her third solo engagement and her first as patron of The Art Room, which helps disadvantaged children gain self-esteem, self-confidence and independence through art therapy. She visited 'Pippa's Room' at Rose Hill, where she joined eight children making puppets from tennis rackets, before dropping in at the secondary school Oxford Spires Academy, where she was presented with a bunch of flowers by 7B pupil Eleanor Oxendale, in a box made in art class and decorated with stamps. The Art Room, which aims to help children with emotional and behavioural difficulties, has 26 classrooms nationwide, including 19 in Oxford and seven in London.

Above: Kate dons an apron at Rose Hill Primary School's Art Room.
Right: meeting pupils at Oxford Spires Academy.

ROTHERFIELD GREYS

St Nicholas' Anglican Church, 1 Church Close, Rotherfield Greys, Oxfordshire RG9 4QD

Prince Charles' stepson Tom Parker Bowles, a cookery writer, married Harpers & Queen fashion journalist Sarah Buys at the Grade II* listed church of St Nicholas in front of a host of royals – the Prince of Wales, Duchess of Cornwall, Princes William and Harry – but Kate turned down an invitation to the 2005 wedding so that she did not fuel media attention. Actress Joanna Lumley, actor Hugh Grant and Rolling Stone Mick Jagger were in the congregation as the bride arrived in a stunning creation by Alexander McQueen. Guests at the reception – at Sara's family estate – were treated to vintage champagne, oysters and a six-tiered wedding cake. St Nicholas' is located in the village of Rotherfield Greys (mentioned in the Domesday Book) and dates from the Norman era although it was 'improved' by the Victorians and little of the original architecture remains. Its most notable feature is the 16th century chapel which contains an ornate tomb dedicated to the Knollys family with effigies of Sir Francis Knollys, a courtier to Henry VIII, Edward VI and Elizabeth I, and his wife Katherine, the daughter of Sir William Carey and Mary Boleyn, who was lady of the bedchamber to her cousin Elizabeth I. Around the sides of the tomb are kneeling effigies of 14 brothers and sisters.

Right: St Nicholas' Church, Rotherfield Greys, where Prince Charles' stepson Tom Parker-Bowles got married.
Above top: the intricately carved chapel.
Above: Above: the ornate Knollys family tomb.

WITNEY

Cogges Manor Farm Museum, Church Lane Witney, Oxfordshire OX28 3LA

Kate was nine years old when she visited Cogges with the 1st St Andrew's Brownies - she and Pippa visited the heritage farmstead in rural Oxfordshire during their pack holiday over Easter 1991. They fed the pigs, tried butter making, watched cooking demonstrations on the kitchen range and dressed up in costumes. Cogges is a beautifully preserved collection of Cotswold stone farm buildings set in its own grounds. The site has been farmed since before the Domesday Book and parts of the manor house date back to the 13th century. Today Cogges is a popular visitor attraction for all the family and a well-known film location for TV and the big screen with shows from the BBC's Countryfile to ITV period dramas Downton Abbey and Arthur & George. Visitors can explore over 15 acres of the manor house and grounds, walled garden, picnic orchard, moated islands and river Windrush walk, or stop for a cream tea in the cafe.

Above and below: the idyllic Cotswold stone manor house and gardens, which Kate and Pippa visited on their Brownie summer camp.

SURREY

EAST MOLESEY

Royal School of Needlework, Apartment 12a, Hampton Court Palace, East Molesey, Surrey KT8 9AU

The year 2012 was a double celebration for the Royal School of Needlework: not only did it celebrate its 140th anniversary, but it received a secret visit from the Duchess of Cambridge to thank the master embroiderers, who worked on her wedding gown. Wearing gloves – and washing their hands every half an hour – they hand stitched the lace, which was influenced by traditional Irish Carrickmacross applique lace in the 1820s (the back of the fabric is as neat as the front). The dress, which was decorated with roses, thistles, daffodils and shamrocks, was so secret that none of the workers knew the name of its designer Sarah Burton, from the fashion label Alexander McQueen. The Royal School of Art Needlework was founded in 1872 by Lady Victoria Welby - its first president was her daughter Princess Christian of Schleswig-Holstein, known as Princess Helena – to revive the art of needlework and provided employment for educated women. It began operating in a room above a bonnet shop in Sloane Street but moved to a purpose-built building in 1903 close to London's Victoria & Albert Museum. The school has long been involved with royal ceremonies – workers created the Coronation regalia for George V in 1910, made the Queen Mother's Robe of State in 1937, the Queen's Coronation train in 1953, embroidered slippers for Prince Charles and a monogrammed lace pillow for Princess Diana for their 1981 wedding and created the balcony hanging at Buckingham Palace for the Queen's Golden Jubilee.

EPSOM

Epsom Downs Racecourse, Epsom Downs, Surrey KT18 5LQ

The 2011 Derby was the first public appearance by the Duke and Duchess of Cambridge since their wedding day. William and Kate turned up at Britain's richest horse race – the Derby Stakes – to support the Queen's horse Carlton House, which was a gift from Sheikh Mohammed, supreme ruler of Dubai. But the favourite was beaten into third place by Pour Moi, much to the Sovereign's disappointment. The Derby, which is a flat race, is open to three-year-old thoroughbred colts and fillies and is run over a distance of one mile, four furlongs and 10 yards (2,343 metres) each June. Its name is synonymous with races around the globe but the Epsom race is the original, originating at a celebration in 1779 after the Oak Stakes. According to legend the host of the party, the 12th Earl of Derby and one of his guests, Sir Charles Bunbury, tossed a coin to decide whom the race would be named after – although it is likely that Bunbury, who was Steward of the Jockey Club, deferred to his host. The inaugural race, held on May 4, 1780, was won by Sir Charles Bunbury's colt Diomed, which collected prize money of £1,065 15s. The Derby has attracted a host of celebrities including author Charles Dickens and artist William Powell Frith, who immortalised the event in his 1858 painting The Derby Day. But the most famous is suffragette Emily Wilding Davison, who threw herself in front of the king's horse Anmer during the 1913 race – she died four days later in Epsom Cottage Hospital.

Top: the traditional art of hand embroidery at the Royal School of Needlework. Above: Epsom Downs Racecourse.

SANDHURST

Royal Military Academy, Sandhurst, Camberley, Surrey GU15 4PQ

It was at the Royal Military Academy Sandhurst that the future commander-in-chief of the British Armed Forces was trained as an officer. His passing-out parade at Sandhurst was the scene of the Duchess of Cambridge's first public appearance: she was watching Second Lieutenant Wales receive his commission, having completed 44-weeks at the academy. Her presence at the 2006 ceremony (with her parents Michael and Carole Middleton and William's private secretary Jamie Lowther-Pinkerton) marked a significant shift in the couple's relationship since they had left university 18 months earlier. Although she was not sitting in the royal stand with the Queen and Prince Charles, her attendance was deemed significant and fuelled speculation that an engagement was imminent (it would be another four years before William proposed). Indeed, the interest in Kate's appearance at the parade was so feverish that ITN went so far as to hire a lip-reader, who reported that the prince's girlfriend had commented afterwards: 'I love the uniform. It's so sexy.' After weeks of intense competition between the nine platoons, William's was named Sovereign's Platoon: the prince had the honour of carrying the Queen's banner during the ceremony - wearing a red sash over his uniform and carrying a rifle, instead of a sword. That night, at the stroke of midnight, as fireworks lit the sky and champagne corks popped, he took part in one final Sandhurst ritual, ripping off the tape covering the pips on his uniform. Founded in the wake of the Second World War, the elite military academy was set up to train regular army officers, replacing two outmoded establishments, the Royal Military College in Sandhurst and the Royal Military Academy in Woolwich, both of which had trained gentlemen cadets. William joined a long list of illustrious recruits to the academy, including the late King Hussein of Jordan, the Sultans of Brunei and Oman, Prince Michael of Kent and Sir Winston Churchill, as well as his younger brother Harry, who was about to enter his third term at Sandhurst (William had to salute him in public for eight months as Harry graduated first). One of 270 cadets, including Alexander Perkins, great-grandson of Sir Winston Churchill, William spent the next five weeks sleeping in a small dormitory, sharing communal washing facilities and surviving what new recruits describe as 'hell on earth'. Banned from leaving the base and allowed only limited use of the telephone, the cadets, who were expected to do their own laundry, iron their shirts and polish their black military boots, rose each day at dawn for a series of intensive drills and endless inspections. They were trained in handling weapons, initially SA80 5.56mm rifles, later 51mm light mortars, light support weapons and Browning 9mm pistols.

Above: Kate's appearance at Sandhurst with her parents sparked engagement rumours – not for the last time.

SUTTON

Royal Marsden Hospital, Downs Road, Sutton, Surrey SM2 5PT

Above: William meets 16-year-old Chloe Drury at the Royal Marsden Hospital.

Almost 30 years after Princess Diana toured the hospital in 1982 on her first solo engagement, the Duke and Duchess of Cambridge opened its new £18 million Oak Centre for children and young people. Despite having not slept all night, because he was on a shift with RAF search and rescue, William and Kate chatted to cancer sufferers at the hospital on their visit in 2011. The Duchess was so touched by meeting nine-year-old Fabian Bate, who was in the middle of four hours of chemotherapy to treat acute lymphoblastic leukaemia for the second time, that she wrote a letter to Fabian, which was among his most treasured possessions when he died on Remembrance Day 2014. The couple also met 16-year-old Ewing's sarcoma sufferer Chloe Drury, who was delighted to shake William's hand. Sadly, Chloe died from the rare bone cancer in 2013, just weeks after her 18th birthday. Opened by the Queen in 1963, the Royal Marsden in Sutton is affiliated to the world-famous Royal Marsden in Fulham - the first hospital in the world dedicated to the study and treatment of cancer.

LONDON &
GREATER LONDON

ART & CULTURE

BAFTA, 195 Piccadilly, London W1J 9LN

Prince William made his first visit to the British Academy of Film and Television Arts in 2013 to launch its campaign Give Something Back, urging its heavyweights to mentor young people wanting to break into the film, TV and gaming industries. The Prince, who is president of BAFTA, road-tested the video game Vacuum Panic, in which he tried to clean his bedroom with a vacuum cleaner. 'I'm not cleaning particularly well,' he told designer Charlie Hutton-Pattermore. 'I'm just going around in circles.' The Royal Family has a long association with BAFTA, which is a listed charity. The Duke of Edinburgh was its first president in 1959 and Prince Philip and the Queen donated royalties from Richard Cawston's documentary Royal Family to the charity in the 1970s enabling it to move to it current Grade II* listed building. The building is not open to the public although it is available for hire.

Previous page: The Palace of Westminster. Top: William launches BAFTA's Give Something Back campaign. Above: the premiere of African Cats.

BFI Southbank, Belvedere Road, South Bank, London SE1 8XT

The Duke and Duchess of Cambridge were guests of honour at the British Film Institute in 2012 when they attended a charity premiere of the wildlife film African Cats in aid of the African conservation charity Tusk. Eighteen months after they got engaged in Africa, a continent they both love, William, who is patron of the charity, and Kate, watched the true story of a pride of lions and family of cheetahs battling for survival. Afterwards the couple mingled with guests such as film maker Guy Ritchie, who is a distant cousin of Kate, Dire Straits guitarist Mark Knopfler and Dragons' Den judge Deborah Meaden, who is a patron of Tusk. CEO Charlie Mayhew said: 'We are now seeing daily reports of elephants being poached across the continent and in South Africa, the country has lost 170 rhinos already this year. William is passionate about Africa and he's very concerned about the current crisis.' Founded in 1933, the BFI opened its first cinema screen after the war. The Queen visited in 2012 to celebrate its anniversary.

London Palladium, Argyll Street, London W1F 7TF

The London Palladium was the 2014 venue for the Royal Variety Show (an annual event in the calendar of the royal family, in aid of the charity the Entertainment Artistes' Benevolent Fund) when The Duke and Duchess of Cambridge were guests of honour for the first time (traditionally the Queen or Prince Charles attends). They met the band One Direction. Afterwards singer Liam Payne confessed: 'It's the most nervous I think I've been.' The London Palladium opened in 1910 but did not host its first royal Variety Performance until 1930, when George V and Queen Mary attended. The theatre became famous for variety in the 1950s with the television show Sunday Night at the London Palladium, which made stars out of its hosts Bruce Forsyth, Norman Vaughan and Jimmy Tarbuck. Since then it has hosted lavish pantomimes and musicals such as Yul Bryner's 1979 show The King and I. Taken over by Andrew Lloyd Webber's Really Useful Theatre company in 2000, its revolving stage was removed in order to stage Chitty Chitty Bang Bang which holds the record as the Palladium's longest-running show.

Above: William chats to veteran comedian Jimmy Tarbuck at the London Palladium.

The O2, Peninsula Square, London SE10 0DX

London's music and entertainment venue The O2 underwent a transformation during the Olympics – and the Duke and Duchess of Cambridge were regular visitors at the temporarily renamed North Greenwich Arena. William and Harry watched the British men's gymnastics team appear in their first Olympics final since 1924 (Louis Smith won a silver medal on the Pommel horse) and Kate saw the vault final of the artistic gymnastics, which was won by the American team. Afterwards she met gold medal winner Jordyn Wieber, who tweeted: 'Can't believe I just met Princess Kate Middleton! She was in the crowd at the competition and she stood up to talk to us! #honored'. It is not the first time the venue has undergone a transformation: it began life as the Dome, where the Queen and Prince Phillip marked the Millennium, before opening in 2007 as The O2. More than 50 million people have visited since then. With 12 steel masts (to represent the months), it covers 80,000 square metres, and is big enough to fit 18,000 double decker buses.

Odeon Leicester Square, 24-26 Leicester Square, London WC2H 7LQ

Prince William has been attending film premieres in Leicester Square since he was a child. His mother, Princess Diana, took him and Prince Harry to the 1991 celebrity premiere of Steven Spielberg's Peter Pan film Hook at the age of nine (they met Dustin Hoffman, Robin Williams and Phil Collins and were given bags of chocolate 'pieces of eight' to eat). Six years later, the two boys attended the premiere of the Spice World: The Movie, with their father, Prince Charles (they met the girls in a private room minutes before the film). But his first attendance at a film premiere without his parents was in 2008 at the James Bond movie Quantum of Solace. He and Prince Harry attended the charity premiere, in aid of Help for Heroes and the Royal British Legion, at the Odeon cinema. Four years later, William and Kate were guests at the premiere of the movie War Horse (Kate was moved to tears) and the following year they attended the film Mandela: Long Walk to Freedom (William and Kate were informed just moments before the screening that Mandela had died). The Odeon Leicester Square opened in 1937 and has hosted more than 700 film premieres.

Above: The O2 looking spectacular at night. Right: a chivalrous William shields Kate from the rain as they arrive at Leicester Square's Odeon for the premiere of War Horse.

Royal Albert Hall, Kensington Gore, London SW7 2AP

The Royal Albert Hall was the venue for the Duke and Duchess of Cambridge's first joint engagement with the Duke and Duchess of Cornwall – a 2011 Take That concert, organised by Gary Barlow, in aid of the Prince's Trust and the Foundation of Prince William and Prince Harry. It was also the scene of a black tie charity ball hosted by William and Kate, who were ambassadors for the Olympic Games, to raise money for the Great Britain team. They watched singer Alfie Boe and Girls Aloud star Kimberley Walsh perform the official Team GB song, One Vision. 'Naturally, I was asked to compete for Team GB in every sport,' William joked, 'but sadly Lord Coe said there were London pigeons with more athletic prowess than me. Anyway, to adopt a famous phrase from Sir Steve Redgrave, if you see me in a pair of Speedos during the Olympics, shoot me. For all of us mere mortals — and I include my brother Harry, still droning on about beating Usain (it never counted, as it was a false start) this is a lifetime opportunity. We will witness an exceptional moment in our island history. The mood in London will be electric, ecstatic, amazing. I just can't wait.' William also attended the Winter Whites Gala - A Spectacular Winter Wonderland Evening of Celebrity, Entertainment and Legendary Masters Tennis, at the Royal Albert Hall, while his wife was recovering at home from morning sickness (she had been taken to hospital with hyperemesis gravidarum). After watching Tim Henman beat Goran Ivanisevic in the veterans' match in aid of Centrepoint, he joked: 'Good to see all those vodka shots at dinner didn't hold you back Tim.' Kate also celebrated her 31st birthday in 2013 in the royal box at the Royal Albert Hall watching the Cirque du Soleil with William and her family, Mike, Carole, Pippa and James, and William joined Prince Charles and Prince Harry there for a Responsible Business Gala Dinner. The Royal Albert Hall was officially opened in 1871 by Queen Victoria in honour of her late husband Prince Albert, who had conceived the idea of the venue. She was so overwhelmed by emotion that her son, the future Edward VII, declared the Royal Albert Hall open. The royal family has its own private entrance near Door 8: it leads to a private room opposite the royal box, which is hung with signed pictures of all the reigning monarchs and their consorts (the entrance was originally at the North Porch's Door 6 when they arrived in carriages). When the Queen, who is patron, attends an event at the Royal Albert Hall, a 12ft-long velvet hammercloth or banner with the royal insignia, embroidered by the Royal School of Needlework, is hung across the front of the royal box.

Above: William and Kate arrive at the Royal Albert Hall for the Our Greatest Team Rises gala ball, a countdown to the 2012 Olympics.

Royal Opera House, Bow Street, London WC2E 9DD

Above left: the ornate Paul Hamlyn Hall glass atrium. Above right: the Royal Opera House.

Prince William stole the show when he made his first appearance at the Royal Opera House in 2010 for the British Academy Film Awards – he even managed to win over avowed republican Vanessa Redgrave when he presented her with a British Academy fellowship. William, who was making his first appearance as the new president of the British Academy of Film and Television Arts, also upstaged actress Kate Winslet, who walked down the red carpet moments after him. 'Britain has been a cultural leader in so many ways not least in its cultural achievements,' he told guests. 'From the days of Shakespeare, to our own Shakespeare in Love, British playwrights, scriptwriters, actors, film makers and now video game designers – have led the way globally, if not always in terms of resource then undoubtedly in talent and innovation. It is quite clear that the same cultural dynamism that so infused the first Elizabethan age still drives the beating heart of British visual arts in this second Elizabethan era.' Originally known as the Theatre Royal, and based in its 19th century building, the Royal Opera House was renamed in 1892, and launched with winter and summer seasons of opera and ballet. But it became a furniture repository during the Great War and was home to a Mecca Dance Hall in World War II. It was only after music publishers Boosey and Hawkes acquired the lease and invited the Sadler's Wells Ballet, under Ninette de Valois, to became its resident ballet company, that the opera house reopened with a 1946 gala performance of The Sleeping Beauty, performed by Margot Fonteyn. As there was no suitable opera company to take up residence, music director Karl Rankl built a company from scratch – the fledgling Covent Garden Opera teamed up with the ballet for a joint production of Purcell's The Fairy Queen, choreographed by Frederick Ashton. Both companies were eventually awarded Royal Charters: the Royal Ballet in 1956, the Royal Opera in 1968. Since then the Royal Opera House has undergone a £178 million three-year renovation. It re-opened in 2000.

BANKS & BROKERS (& THE LAW)

BGC, 1 Churchill Place, London W14 5RD

Princes William and Harry joined brokers in the heart of London's financial district to raise money for charity – and negotiated the biggest deal of the day. The two brothers squared up to each other on the trading floor of BGC Brokers' for its annual charity day, in memory of its 658 employees, who died at the World Trade Centre on 9/11, before landing the £19 billion foreign currency trade. Profits from the day were donated to their nominated charities: SkillForce and WellChild. William (patron of SkillForce) and Harry (patron of WellChild) joined celebrities such as singer Rod Stewart, musician Ronnie Wood, comedian Jennifer Saunders, actress Thandie Newton and Baywatch star David Hasselhoff, to hit the phones in aid of charity. They raised laughs as they switched from desk to desk, bantering with each other as they negotiated – at one point Harry told William: 'Stop flirting and get on with it.' The first BGC Day in London was launched in 2004 when world champion motorcycle trials rider Dougie Lampkin, rode his bike through the ground floor lobby and up to the trading floors of the Canary Wharf office, jumping turnstiles and desks on his way. Since then, the BGC Charity Day has raised more than £59 billion.

Clifford Chance, 10 Upper Bank Street, London E14 5JJ

The Duchess of Cambridge almost had a 'Marilyn Monroe' moment when she arrived at the legal firm Clifford Chance and bent down to accept a posy. Her skirt, which, unlike the Queen's, was not weighed down with lead curtain weights, caught in the wind. Kate, who was supposed to still be on maternity leave, was in Canary Wharf to attend a schools' forum about cyber bullying and sexting. Organised by the charity Place2Be, of which she is royal patron, she joined volunteers and children in the conference theatre. Place2Be aims to steer children 'away from a downward spiral of low aspirations, truancy and exclusion from school, so that they can achieve their potential, both in and outside the classroom and face brighter futures as they deserve'. The charity works with more than 200 schools across the country.

HSBC, 78 St James' Street, London SW1A 1EJ

Prince William's first experience with the financial sector was in 2005 when he did a week's work experience shadowing bankers at HSBC. The prince swapped his wellies for a pinstriped suit to spend a week working with the bank's Charities Investment Services team in St James's Street, just around the corner from Clarence House, before commuting to its investment arm in Canary Wharf. He also spent some time at the Bank of England, learning how it sets interest rates, and visited the London Stock Exchange, Lloyd's of London, the Financial Services Authority and the Queen's lawyers, Farrer & Co. Three years later, William returned to HSBC as patron of the homeless charity Centrepoint – it was his first patronage, following in the footsteps of his mother Princess Diana, who had taken him and Harry to visit hostels as children – he attended HSBC for a reception to mark the launch of the charity's 40th anniversary year. He was back again at HSBC in 2010, as patron of Tusk Trust, meeting supporters and launching its 20th anniversary.

Above: William launches the 20th Anniversary of Tusk Trust at HSBC.

BARS & CLUBS

Boujis, 43 Thurloe Street, London SW7 2LQ

The romance between the Duke and Duchess of Cambridge was played out at private members' club Boujis, a favourite haunt of the young royals. William and Kate were regulars at the club when they first left university - drawn by its exclusivity and discretion (and their own private 'Brown Room' where they downed the signature Crack Baby cocktail – a mixture of vodka, passion-fruit juice, Chambord and champagne in a test tube). Then run by Norman Parkinson's grandson Jake Parkinson-Smith, nobody got behind the Boujis rope unless they had serious connections.

Loulou's, 5 Hertford Street, London W1J 7SD

The Duke and Duchess of Cambridge made a rare visit to a nightclub as a married couple in 2012 after the funeral of his beloved nanny Olga Powell. He and Kate, who had been on a solo tour of Newcastle, were reunited at the exclusive private members' club Loulou's, arriving unexpectedly to join Pippa Middleton and Princess Eugenie on the dancefloor. The party also included Eugenie's boyfriend Jack Brooksbank, and Jemima Khan and Zach Goldsmith, whose stepbrother Robin Birley owns the club. He is the son of Mark Birley, who created the famous Annabel's club for Jemima and Zach's mother Lady Annabel Vane-Tempest-Stewart.

Mahiki, 1 Dover Street, London W1S 4LD

Owned by nightclub impresario Piers Adam, club promoter Nick House and businessman David Phelps, and designed to resemble a Polynesian beach bar, Mahiki was a favourite of the Duke and Duchess before they married. William's friend Guy Pelly was the club's marketing director, and Henry Conway, the flamboyant self-styled 'Queen of Sloanes', ran Thursday-night parties there. So it was there that William went to drown his sorrows in 2007 after his temporary split from Kate. The party ran up a bill of £4,700 working their way through the Mahiki Trail cocktail menu. At one point, William is supposed to have yelled, 'I'm free!', before performing his own version of the robot dance goal celebration that Liverpool striker Peter Crouch had shown him during a World Cup training session.

Raffles, 287 King's Road, London SW3 5EW

Another favourite haunt, the private members' club Raffles describes itself as 'one of the last bastions of decadence and debauchery' – although William and Kate behaved impeccably. Named after colonial mogul Sir Thomas Stamford Raffles, and founded in 1967 by restaurateur Peter Evans, who was a close friend of Princess Margaret, the club was the stamping ground of the Rolling Stones, Eric Clapton and Vivienne Westwood as well as the royal family. The Queen herself attended the club in the 1970s with Prince Charles and Princess Anne.

Roof Gardens, 99 Kensington High Street, London W8 5SA

When Sir Richard Branson invited the Duchess of Cambridge to a party at the Roof Gardens to celebrate the start of Wimbledon in 2006, she was bound to go – she is a huge tennis fan. Although William was unable to attend, because he was on a military training exercise in Wales, Kate arrived in a group, which included Sir Richard's daughter Holly. She spent the night dancing with Guy Pelly and chatting to tennis player Maria Sharapova. The Roof Gardens, is set in 1.5 acres of grounds with fully-grown oaks and fruit trees, a flowing stream, stocked with fish and wildlife and resident flamingos. It is London's only rooftop Private Members Club with a dress code which states 'no effort, no entry'.

Tonteria, 7-12 Sloane Square, London SW1W 8EG

Princes William and Harry were guests of honour at the Mexican tapas and tequila nightspot Tonteria in 2013 for Thomas van Straubenzee's stag do. William, who was wearing a bright orange Greys cap, emblazoned with the words 'Born to fish' partied with Thomas, known as 'Van', before his wedding to Lady Melissa Percy. He kept his head down as the group left the club through the back door at 1.15am. Tonteria (which translates as 'something of little consequence') is owned by the princes' close friend Guy Pelly, who reputedly organised his stag do, and business partner Marc Burton – they met at Mahiki, where they were entrusted with looking after VIPs, and went on to open Public and Tonteria. Tonteria offers an early-evening Tapas menu - with sharing cocktails including the 'Mayan Pyramid', 'Lucky Luchador' and 'Tequila Slammer', delivered in skulls by waiters in authentic costume – and a nightspot table by the dance floor. Its interior, with its hand-painted tiles and large Mexican plants, is inspired by the Latin American city and a toy train delivers tequila shots to people lazing in hammocks.

Whisky Mist, 35 Hertford Street, London W1J 7SD

Whisky Mist is reportedly where Paris Hilton made an unsuccessful pass at Prince William in 2008 (although the story needs to be taken with a pinch of salt). Renowned for its rich and opulent décor, it pays homage to all things Scottish with suits of armour, coats of arms, crested tartan wallpaper, whisky barrels and a majestic stag. Its signature cocktail (infused with amber and honey) is served in a pewter, steel, leather and horn vessel by attendants in tartan uniforms.

BRITAIN'S HERITAGE

Australia House, Strand, London WC2B 4LA

He is well known in Australia but the name of Captain Matthew Flinders was barely recognised in his native Britain - until Prince William unveiled his memorial sculpture. William paid tribute to the 27-year-old cartographer, who was the first person to circumnavigate Australia, during a 2014 ceremony at Australia House. Unveiling the 6ft bronze memorial, designed by sculptor Mark Richards, he said he was honoured to recognise the man who did 'far more than anyone else to place Australia – quite literally – on the map'. The statue, of Flinders kneeling over a map of Australia with his compass and his cat Trim, has now been erected at Euston Station, where he is believed to have been buried (William was given a miniature version of the statue). William also unveiled a commemorative Matthew Flinders locomotive nameplate for one of the Pendolino trains, which runs between Euston and Glasgow. Captain Flinders, who was a naval officer, discovered that New South Wales and Western Australia were one giant land mass – he is also credited with giving the country its name when he drew his '1804 General Chart of Terra Australis'. Australia House is the oldest Australian diplomatic mission and the longest continuously-occupied foreign mission in London. George V (accompanied by the Queen and Princess Mary) laid its foundation stone in 1913 but he did not officially open the building until the end of World War I.

Banqueting House, Whitehall, London SW1A 2ER

The Duke and Duchess of Cambridge visited one of London's most historic buildings in 2005 when they attended a charity ball. They joined friends for the £80-a-head black tie party, in aid of Cancer Research, at the building where Charles I was executed for treason. But the couple sparked speculation about the state of their relationship by hosting separate tables and barely dancing together – despite the fact that etiquette suggests they should work the room. Banqueting House was built on land originally owned by the Archbishops of York – they built the nearby 14th century York Place, close to the King's palace at Westminster. (The Venetian ambassador described the town house, as 'a very fine palace, where one traverses eight rooms before reaching the audience chamber'.) When Thomas Wolsey became Archbishop of York, he began to extend the building and Henry VIII became a regular visitor. But when their relationship disintegrated, he was stripped of all his assets and the king took over York Place, renaming it 'Whitehall' and building tennis courts, a tiltyard for tournaments and a cockpit on a plot of land opposite the palace. On his death, the building spanned 23 acres and was the largest royal palace in Europe. Whitehall's current Banqueting House was designed by Inigo Jones in the 17th century – its crowning glory is the ceiling, commissioned by Charles I and painted by Flemish artist Sir Peter Paul Rubens (he was paid £3,000 and a heavy gold chain). The last king to live at Whitehall Palace was James II – he used Banqueting House as a furniture store.

Top: William pays tribute to Captain Matthew Flinders at the unveiling of his statue. Above: Banqueting House, one of London's most historic buildings.

Cenotaph, Whitehall, London SW1A 2BX

The Duchess of Cambridge attended her first Remembrance Sunday ceremony at the Cenotaph in 2011, following royal tradition by wearing two scarlet poppies. She stood on a balcony overlooking the Cenotaph with the Duchess of Cornwall and the Countess of Wessex (protocol dictates that only royals – apart from Prince Philip - watch from the ground while spouses look down from the balconies above). Kate watched members of the royal family lay wreaths at the memorial, followed by party leaders and Commonwealth representatives. The Cenotaph, which means 'empty tomb' in Greek, was originally built as a temporary structure to commemorate the dead on the first anniversary of the Armistice in 1919. But, after it was spontaneously covered with wreaths to the dead and missing in the Great War, Prime Minister Lloyd George commissioned a permanent structure. Designed by Sir Edwin Lutyens, and made from Portland stone, it was unveiled in 1920, with the inscription 'The Glorious Dead'.

Goldsmiths' Hall, Foster Lane, London EC2V 6BN

The Duke and Duchess of Cambridge celebrated at Goldsmiths' Hall in 2012 after two army teams retraced the exact routes of the race to the South Pole by British explorer Sir Robert Falcon Scott and Norwegian Roald Amundsen. Prince William, who was patron of the Scott-Amundsen Centenary Race to the South Pole, toasted the six officers, who made the first unassisted attempt to reach the South Pole since Scott perished in the Antarctic, raising money for the Royal British Legion. The six officers had set off on November 11, 2011, from the Bay of Whales and Cape Evans (the respective starting points for the Amundsen and Scott expeditions) carrying their own food and fuel across the ice on sledges weighing 140kg apiece. Both teams arrived at the South Pole the following January. Designed by Philip Hardwick in 1835, Goldsmith's Hall, is one of London's hidden treasures (it narrowly escaped destruction during World War II when a bomb exploded inside it).

Top: the Duke of Cambridge lays a wreath at the Cenotaph. Middle: Kate at Goldsmith's Hall. Above: Guildhall.

Guildhall London, Gresham Street, London, EC2V 7HH

When he became patron of the 2008 Lord Mayor's Appeal, Prince William was guest of honour at a Sporting Heroes Dinner at the Guildhall and arrived wearing a Help for Heroes coloured wristband. The Prince was launching the Lord Mayor's Appeal, a fundraiser for two health charities Wellbeing of Women and Orbis. 'Becoming involved in this way is particularly special for me because of the past association and commitment of my mother, Diana, Princess of Wales, to Wellbeing of Women,' he said 'The vital work of Orbis in helping to save sight in India and other regions of the developing world was also endorsed by my mother and is of particular interest to me.' Six months later William returned to the Guildhall for a dinner to mark the end of the appeal year. The grade I listed building Guildhall, which was built in the 15th century, is home to the City of London Corporation and is a setting for state banquets and other royal events.

Horse Guards Parade, Whitehall, London SW1A 2AX

The Trooping of the Colour ceremony in 2011 marked a first in the lives of the Duke and Duchess of Cambridge – it was the first state occasion Kate had attended since the royal wedding and was the first time William had taken part in the parade on horseback. Kate watched proudly as her husband made his debut escorting the Queen for her official Birthday Parade (he rode a grey called Wellesley). She travelled to the pageant in a carriage with the Duchess of Cornwall and Prince Harry and saw the ceremony from the Horse Guards building. Originally the Palace of Whitehall's tiltyard, where Henry VIII held jousting tournaments, Horse Guards Parade was once the British Army headquarters (the Duke of Wellington was based there). Fronted by the Horse Guards building, designed by George II's architect William Kent, the vast parade ground is best known for the Trooping of the Colour ceremony, where the Queen takes her salute on her official birthday. The Horse Guards building marks the official entrance to St James' Palace and Buckingham Palace. It is guarded by two members of the Queen's Life Guard (mounted troopers from the Household Cavalry) who change every hour – an official Changing of the Guard ceremony takes place at 11am on weekdays and 10am on Sundays. Horse Guards Parade also hosted the beach volleyball during the 2012 London Olympics – watched by Prince Harry.

Middle Temple Inn, Middle Temple Lane, London EC4Y 9AT

It was at Middle Temple Inn that the Duchess of Cambridge made a joke about her catwalk appearance in her lingerie while she was at St Andrews University. She and William were attending a 2012 fundraising dinner to raise £100 million for the university and mark its 600th anniversary when, chatting to a student, she said: 'I hope you weren't involved in the fashion show. You never know what you are going to be asked to wear.' They were making their second joint visit to Middle Temple Inn, one of four ancient Inns of Court, where newly-qualified barristers are called to the English Bar, which means they can stand up in court. A month earlier they unveiled a legal scholarship, set up in their name for disadvantaged students, building on the legacy of the Queen Mother and Princess Diana, who already have memorial scholarships. William was called to the bar as an honorary barrister in 2009 (he promised not to practice) and is the sixth member of the Royal family to become a Royal Bencher, following in the footsteps of the Queen Mother, called in 1944, and his mother Diana, Princess of Wales, called in 1988. The Prince also attended a 100 Women in Hedge Funds Philanthropic Initiatives gala dinner at Middle Temple in 2010 - after he and Prince Harry were appointed patrons for three years (they chose Centrepoint, the Child Bereavement Charity and SkillForce as their charities). The Inns of Court originated as hostels and schools for student lawyers in the 13th century – its name derived from the Knights Templar, which owned its site – but is now the home to barristers' chambers. With its cobbled streets, historic buildings and gas lighting, the Inns of Court are a popular venue for film producers (William Shakespeare's Twelfth Night had its first recorded performance in Middle Temple Hall in 1602).

Top: William and Prince Charles on horseback at the Trooping of the Colour. Above: the historic Middle Temple Inn.

Tower of London, London EC3N 4AB

Above: a sea of poppies at the Tower of London became the most iconic image of 2014. Opposite: William, Kate and Harry pay their respects to the fallen soldiers of World War I.

The scene of the Duke and Duchess of Cambridge in a sea of poppies at the Tower of London was the most memorable image of 2014. William, Kate and Harry visited the memorial to commemorate the 100th anniversary of World War I and each installed a ceramic poppy. The installation was the brainchild of ceramic artist Paul Cummins after he visited Derbyshire Archives and came across a living will, written by an unknown soldier, which included the moving line 'Blood Swept Lands and Seas of Red'. He approached Historic Royal Palaces, which runs the Tower of London, and was commissioned to create 888,246 ceramic flowers to mark each of the Commonwealth soldiers who died in the war. The Tower of London dates back to the 11th century, when William the Conqueror defeated Harold at the Battle of Hastings and built its central White Tower, the great stone keep that dominates the castle today, which was protected by Roman walls. Never intended as a royal residence, it became renowned in Tudor times when Henry VIII imprisoned his chancellor Sir Thomas More and two of his wives, Anne Boleyn and Catherine Howard, in the Tower before they were executed. The Tower of London is also the home to the Crown Jewels, which are guarded by Beefeaters.

CHURCHES & CATHEDRALS

Guards' Chapel, Wellington Barracks, Birdcage Walk, London SW1E 6HQ

The Guards' Chapel was the venue for the 2009 wedding of Prince William's close friend Nicholas van Cutsem, a Life Guard in the Household Cavalry. He married Alice Hadden-Patten, an event manager, (her brother is the actor Harry Hadden-Patten) at the chapel, in Wellington Barracks. Both Prince William and Prince Harry, then in the Blues and Royals, were ushers, while the Duchess of Cambridge was among the guests. The only military chapel in London, the Guards' Chapel is the spiritual home of the seven Regiments of the Household Division: The Household Cavalry -The Life Guards and The Blues and Royals - and the Guards Division, made up from five Regiments of the Foot Guards, Grenadiers, Coldstream, Scots, Irish Guards and Welsh Guards. Originally built in 1838, it was destroyed, in 1944, by a flying bomb, which killed 121 people, including the officiating chaplain (the altar candles defiantly remained burning). After the war, a hut was erected within the ruined walls (services were resumed on Christmas Day 1945) and a war memorial cloister was erected between the chapel and Birdcage Walk. A new chapel, containing the original mosaic-decorated apse, font and cross, which survived the bomb, and the war memorial cloisture, was dedicated in 1963.

Holy Trinity Church, Uxbridge Road, Southall UB1 3HH

It was two months after the Queen's Coronation, that the Duchess of Cambridge's grandparents Ronald and Dorothy Goldsmith got married in this church in Southall. At that time Ronald was working as a lorry driver for his brother-in-law Bill Tomlinson's haulage company; Dorothy, who had two matrons of honour and two bridesmaids, was working as a shop assistant in Dorothy Perkins.

Above left: the Guards'Chapel.
Left: Ronald and Dorothy Goldsmith on their wedding day.

St Luke's Church, St Luke's Crypt, Sydney Street, London SW3 6NH

The young royals have been regulars in the congregation at St Luke's Church since it became the venue for a charity carol concert in remembrance of their close friend Henry van Straubenzee, who died in a car crash at the age of 18. The Duchess of Cambridge was spotted in a pew at the church during the 2010 fundraiser in aid of the Henry van Straubenzee Memorial Fund, which educates disadvantaged children in Uganda. Prince William, who is a patron of the charity, was unable to attend because he was in Switzerland with David Cameron and David Beckham promoting England's World Cup bid. But he and Prince Harry turned up at the service in 2014 and paid an emotional tribute to their childhood companion. In a rare joint address, the princes stood side by side as they spoke of the young man they remembered as their 'very special friend'. Harry, who was at the pulpit, described Henry as a 'Polzeath surfing legend and ladies' man with whom we shared so many special memories'. 'I'm sure you understand when I say most of those memories are not suitable for public consumption let alone in the house of God,' he added. William, across the aisle at the Lectern, then struck a more somber tone. 'We are, of course, here to remember Henry,' he said. 'He was a friend to many people here and a very special friend to us, who we share so many happy childhood memories with. Henry would be amazed that his charity is giving so many children a chance in life. He certainly enjoyed his.' Afterwards Ellie Goulding performed the song 'Have Yourself a Merry Little Christmas' (she has also sung it for President Obama). Designed by James Savage, the Grade I listed 19th century St Luke's Church is one of the earliest Gothic Revival churches in London. (It cost £40,000 and was designed to seat 2,500 people). Author Charles Dickens was married at the church in 1836, two days after the publication of the first instalment of the Pickwick Papers, to Catherine Hogarth. And, in 1996, the church appeared in the film 101 Dalmations.

Right: St Luke's Church in the heart of Chelsea.

St Paul's Cathedral, St Paul's Churchyard, London EC4M 8AD

London's most famous cathedral, this Christopher Wren masterpiece was chosen by Prince William's parents for their 1981 wedding ceremony. Lady Diana Spencer, who was wearing a £9,000 ivory taffeta and antique lace gown with a 25ft train, designed by David and Elizabeth Emmanuel, arrived in a glass coach and walked down the aisle on the arm of her father, Earl Spencer. (it took her three and a half minutes). Watched by 3,500 guests, she and Prince Charles then made their vows before walking out of the cathedral to the sound of Elgar's 'Pomp and Circumstance'. The streets were lined with 600,000 people (another 750 million watched on television) as they travelled back to Buckingham Palace in an open-topped landau, emerging on the balcony shortly afterwards for the long-awaited kiss. Twenty-seven years later Princes William and Harry returned to the cathedral for a sunset pageant in honour of the City Salute Appeal, in aid of Help for Heroes and the Soldiers, Sailors, Airmen and Families Association, of which they were both patrons. They watched a fly past and aerial display by the RAF, as well as a drill display by the Queen's Colour Squadron, and a light show projected onto the cathedral. The two royals, both in the Household Cavalry's Blues and Royals, wrote in the programme: 'We are both currently enjoying the privilege of seeing at first hand the simply remarkable job which the men and women of our Armed Forces do. Their professionalism is coupled with quite extraordinary personal qualities of courage, resilience, modesty, and humour - qualities which they display in good times and in bad, and which are humbling and inspiring beyond measure.' That year, Prince William also attended a concert at the cathedral, to mark the end of his year as patron of The Lord Mayor's Appeal. He listened to classical violinist Jennifer Pike, who won the BBC Young Musician of the Year competition when she was 12, perform Mendelssohn's violin concerto in E minor, accompanied by the Philharmonia Orchestra. St Paul's Cathedral was designed by one of Britain's most famous architects Sir Christopher Wren to replace the cathedral which was destroyed by the Great Fire of London. (Its final stone was laid by his son Christopher and Edward Strong, son of the master mason). Inside there are memorials to national heroes such as Wellington and Lawrence of Arabia; poets John Donne and William Blake and scientist Alexander Fleming. As well as the royal wedding, the cathedral has been the occasion for both national mourning and celebration. Both Winston Churchill and Margaret Thatcher's funerals were held at St Paul's as was the Queen's Diamond Jubilee Service, which was attended by the Duke and Duchess of Cambridge.

Above: St Paul's Cathedral.

Westminster Abbey, 20 Deans Yard, London SW1P 3PA

When the Duke and Duchess of Cambridge married at Westminster Abbey on April 29, 2011, they followed in illustrious footsteps: the Abbey had been the setting for every Coronation since William I in 1066 and had hosted 16 royal weddings including those of William's great-grandfather George VI and the Queen. The couple was pronounced man and wife at precisely 11.20am by the Archbishop of Canterbury, Dr Rowan Williams. Twenty minutes earlier, the tension was palpable as Prince William stood at the altar in the red tunic of the Irish Guards, of which he is honorary colonel, beside his best man, brother Prince Harry, in the uniform of his regiment the Blues and Royals. Cheers broke out as Kate emerged from her car in an ivory silk and lace gown by Sarah Burton at Alexander McQueen, inspired by the late Grace Kelly. Her 'something borrowed' was a 1936 Cartier Halo tiara, loaned to her by the Queen; her 'something new' a pair of diamond earrings, created by the jeweller Robinson Pelham, inspired by the Middleton family's new coat of arms (acorns and oak leaves) and given to her by her parents. The bride walked up the aisle, lined with a red carpet and an avenue of trees, on her father's arm, to the strains of the Coronation anthem I Was Glad, by Sir Charles Hubert Hastings Parry, from Psalm 122. Her sister Pippa, who was maid of honour, (later dubbed her 'Royal Hotness' because of her derrière) carried the 2.7 metre train. There were four bridesmaids – Lady Louise Windsor, the seven-year-old daughter of the Earl and Countess of Wessex, the Hon Margarita Armstrong-Jones, eight-year-old daughter of Viscount and Viscountess Linley, Grace van Cutsem, three-year-old daughter of friend Hugh van Cutsem and Eliza Lopes, the three-year-old granddaughter of the Duchess of Cornwall. The page boys were William Lowther-Pinkerton, ten-year-old son of William's private secretary Major Jamie Lowther-Pinkerton, and Tom Pettifer, eight-year-old son of William and Harry's former nanny Tiggy. William did not turn round until Kate reached the altar but Harry gave him a running commentary. According to a lip reader, he told her she looked 'beautiful' as she joined him at the altar, before joking to his father-in-law 'just a small family affair'. The ceremony, watched by 1,900 guests, ran smoothly but there was a tiny blip – when William struggled to place the Welsh gold wedding band on his bride's finger. Kate's brother James read the lesson Romans 12: 1-2, 9-18, the congregation sang Jerusalem and there were classical compositions by Elgar, Britten and Vaughan Williams. It would be another two years until William and Kate returned to the Abbey – for the 60th anniversary of the Queen's Coronation. Built in the medieval era, Britain's 'West Minster', as it was once known to distinguish it from St Paul's (East Minster), is a shrine to history's great: many notable people are interred in the cathedral, including royals, heads of state, authors and poets. But one particular grave, close to the west door, has become a place of pilgrimage – visiting heads of state invariably lay a wreath on the grave of the Unknown Warrior.

Above: Westminster Abbey is one of the world's most famous churches and a must to visit when in London.

Above: the new Duke and Duchess of Cambridge leave Westminster Abbey.

HOSPITALS

Great Ormond Street Hospital, Great Ormond Street, London WC1N 3JH

The royal family has had a relationship with Great Ormond Street hospital for three centuries and both Prince William and Prince Harry have been treated there. Harry had a hernia operation at the hospital in 1988, when he was three years old, while an eight-year-old William was treated there in 1990, when he was accidentally hit on the head with a golf club by a school friend - tests at the hospital's specialist brain unit showed he had a depressed fracture of the skull. Princess Diana stayed at the hospital while he had an operation while Prince Charles, assured that his son would be fine, went to a long-standing engagement. Great Ormond Street Hospital was founded in 1852 – it celebrated its centenary a week after the Queen's Coronation. Its first patron was Queen Victoria, who contributed £100 to the hospital, and donated linen, games and food – she even sent a batch of toys, which she bought on a trip to Germany. When its new building opened in 1875, the future Edward VII and his bride Princess Alexandra laid the foundation stone and some of its wards – the Victoria and Alexandra ward - were named after the royal family. After his mother's death Edward VII took over as patron of the hospital – as did his son George V and grandson George VI – but it was his granddaughter Princess Mary, later Princess Royal, who had a special relationship with the hospital – she trained to be a nurse, working two days a week in the Alexandra ward, and was a lifelong supporter of the hospital. The Queen first visited Great Ormond Street in 1952, the year of her coronation, when it was celebrating its centenary and has been back on both her Silver and Golden Jubilees (when the hospital was celebrating its 125th and 150th anniversaries). Prince Charles and Princess Diana were patrons of its 1986 Wishing Well appeal and Diana was president of the hospital from 1989 until her death – her final official visit was to open its new renal ward in 1997. Prince Charles returned in 2006 with the Duchess of Cornwall to visit its new Octav Bonar wing. The hospital is not open to members of the public.

Left: Great Ormond Street Children's Hospital has 300-year-old links with the royal family.

King Edward VII Hospital, Beaumont Street, London W1G 6AA

Located in a quiet street in Marylebone, the King Edward VII Hospital is the hospital of choice for the royal family: when the Duchess of Cambridge was admitted in 2012 with hyperemesis gravidarum (extreme morning sickness) she was the latest in a long line of royal patients to be treated there. The Queen Mother had a fishbone removed from her throat, a cataract removed from her left eye and two hip operations at the hospital; the Queen had surgery to remove a torn cartilage from her right knee and lesions from her face; and Prince Philip was treated there for a bladder infection after the Diamond Jubilee pageant. Both Prince Charles and the Duchess of Cornwall have also been admitted (Charles for a hernia op and Camilla for a hysterectomy). But, tragically, Kate's admittance led to a chain of events, which could not have been foreseen. Two Australian DJs made a hoax call to the hospital, posing as the Queen and Prince Charles, and nurse Jacintha Saldanha, who put them through to the ward, killed herself in shame. Afterwards the hospital paid tribute to a 'first-class nurse who cared diligently for hundreds of patients.' The King Edward VII hospital was founded in 1899 by Agnes Keyser, a mistress of Edward VII, then Prince of Wales, and her sister Fanny. They turned their home at 17 Grosvenor Crescent into a hospital for sick and wounded officers returning from the Boer War. Edward VII was the hospital's first patron. Its current patron, the Queen, officially opened its current premises in 1948.

Top: Kate leaves hospital with William after being treated for severe morning sickness.
Above: The Royal Marsden Hospital, Fulham.

The Royal Marsden, Fulham Road, London SW3 6JJ

Prince William took on his mother's mantle in 2007 when he became president of The Royal Marsden Hospital, Britain's leading cancer hospital – Princess Diana held the position from 1989 until her death in 1997. The following year a fire swept through the hospital, destroying its theatre suite and William paid his first visit to meet staff who helped with the evacuation. Five years later the prince returned to the hospital to see two live operations – he donned scrubs to watch a pioneering procedure to remove a bladder tumour and some breast reconstruction surgery. He was also shown the hospital's CyberKnife radiotherapy machine. When asked how he had fared, he held his tummy and replied: 'Good. Still standing.' The Royal Marsden Hospital was founded in 1851 by Dr William Marsden, who was devastated by the death of his wife Elizabeth Ann from the disease. Known as the Free Cancer Hospital, it was the first hospital in the world dedicated to the study and treatment of cancer. The foundation stone of the current hospital was laid by Baroness Coutts in 1859 and the hospital was opened in 1862. It was renamed The Royal Marsden in 1954. In 1991 it became the first NHS hospital to be awarded the Queen's Award for Technology for its work on drug development.

St Mary's Hospital, Praed Street, London W2 1NY

Prince George became the tenth royal baby to be born at St Mary's Hospital, when he was delivered at 16.24pm on July 22, 2013 (the announcement was displayed on an easel outside Buckingham Palace). Prince William, who himself was born at the hospital, was at the Duchess of Cambridge's bedside when she gave birth to their son, who weighed eight pounds six ounces, in the Lindo Wing. He was delivered by a team of doctors including the Queen's former surgeon-gynaecologist Marcus Setchell, her current surgeon-gynaecologist Alan Farthing and the Royal Household's surgeon gynaecologist Dr Guy Thorpe Beeston. Before the establishment of the NHS, St Mary's was a voluntary hospital, which treated the 'deserving poor'. Its Lindo Wing, which was funded by wealthy businessman Frank Lindo, was opened by the Queen Mother in 1937, with 66 'paybeds' – it charged 'patients of moderate means' seven guineas a week. When the NHS took over St Mary's, the Lindo Wing became the hospital's private ward, treating patients such as Prime Minister Clement Attlee, who had meetings from his hospital bed in 1951 with Aneurin Bevan and Harold Wilson about prescription charges (they both resigned over the issue). Sir George Pinker, who was the Queen's gynaecologist and obstetrician between 1973 until 1990, was responsible for moving royal births from palaces to a hospital setting. He delivered nine royal babies in the Lindo Wing, including William and Harry, their cousins Zara and Peter Phillips and the children of the Duchess of Gloucester and Princess Michael of Kent. The wing was given an extensive refurbishment in June 2012 and now provides what it claims is the 'highest quality of care', whether patients experience a 'straightforward' or complex pregnancy. Kate is believed to have taken a deluxe suite of two rooms, costing £6,265 for the delivery and accommodation. Her room had a satellite television, Wi-Fi, a radio, a safe and a fridge. The hospital also has a special care section, the Winnicott Baby Unit, which Prince William visited in 2006, cradling two premature babies, one weighing just five pounds.

Top: William and Kate leave St Mary's Hospital with Prince George.

HOTELS

Claridge's, Brook Street, London W1K 4HR

The Duke and Duchess of Cambridge have attended two glittering social occasions at Claridge's (where Kate Moss celebrated her 30th birthday) - a private dinner and a star-studded charity awards ceremony. Their first visit to the Mayfair hotel, which is known as a 'jewel' of the Art Deco movement, was in 2012 for a meeting of the Thirty Club, founded in 1905 for the

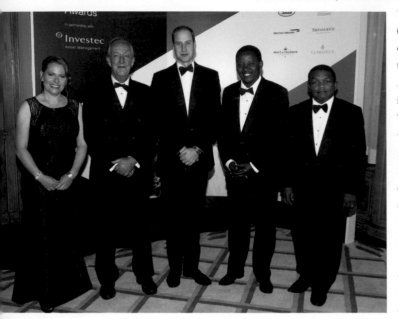

'betterment of advertising' and named after its 30 founders (known as 'peacocks'). William was a guest speaker at the dinner (dubbed a 'great flurry of feathers'), following in the footsteps of his grandfather Prince Philip, aunt Princess Anne and mother Princess Diana. Two years later William returned to the hotel for the Tusk Conservation Awards. The prince, who is the charity's royal patron, mingled with guests such as opera singer Katherine Jenkins, impressionist Rory Bremner, singer Camilla Kerslake, and Dragon's Den star Deborah Meaden, who is a patron of the charity. He then presented the first prize to Madagascan conservationist Herizo Andrianandrasana, who worked for The Durrell Wildlife Conservation Trust, founded by English naturalist, author and TV presenter Gerald Durrell. 'The work of this year's finalists serves to illustrate some of our greatest conservation challenges: dramatic loss of lion; poaching of elephant and rhino; deforestation; and the critical need for community involvement,' said William.

'Wildlife rangers are the men and women at the frontline of the battle – and it is a battle – to save some of the world's most iconic species.' Since opening its doors in 1856, Claridge's has been one of London's most exclusive hotels, hosting royals and celebrities such as Audrey Hepburn, Cary Grant and Bing Crosby (when Katherine Hepburn stayed there she used the staff entrance as trousers were banned in the lobby). The hotel first became a home-from-home for the royals in 1860 when Queen Victoria visited her friend Empress Eugenie of France, beginning a tradition which continues to this day. During World War II, Claridges's became a haven for exiled royalty and heads of state – in 1945 Winston Church declared suite 212 Yugoslavian territory for a day and a clod of Yugoslavian earth was laid under the bed, so that Crown Prince Alexander II could be born on his own country's soil. In 1947, before the wedding of the Queen, a harassed diplomat telephoned Claridge's and asked to speak to the King. 'Certainly sir,' was the response, 'but which one?'

Above: William with the Tusk Conservation Awards finalists 2014
L to R: Amy Dickman, Richard Bonham, David Kuria, Herizo Andrianandrasana.
Opposite: William and Kate arrive at Claridge's for a meeting of the Thirty Club.

The Dorchester, 53 Park Lane, London W1K 1QA

The Duchess of Cambridge caused controversy in 2014 when she breached a ban of The Dorchester hotel for the marriage of her cousin Adam Middleton and interior designer Rebecca Poynton. Kate sneaked into the underground car park in a blacked-out people carrier to meet her family at the wedding in the hotel's penthouse and pavilion. The Dorchester, has hosted royals, celebrities and politicians, since it opened its doors in 1931 – its celebrated Oliver Messel Suite was created by the theatrical designer in the 1950s. General Eisenhower set up his headquarters at the Dorchester during World War II, to plan the Normandy invasion; the Queen attended a dinner party at the hotel, the day before her engagement was announced in 1947; and Prince Philip celebrated his stag night there on the eve of the wedding. But in recent years the hotel has been the focus of a worldwide boycott over its ties to the Sultanate of Brunei, which increased the punishment for homosexuality from a ten-year prison sentence to death by stoning.

The Goring, 15 Beeston Place, London SW1W 0JW

Rumoured to have had a secret tunnel to Buckingham Palace, The Goring hotel in London was where the Duchess of Cambridge spent her last night as a single woman. She stayed in the Royal Suite before her 2011 wedding to Prince William and it was on its steps that the world first caught a glimpse of her Sarah Burton for Alexander McQueen wedding gown. The Goring was the first hotel in London to have en-suite bathrooms when it opened in 1910 by Otto Richard Goring (the price of rooms was 7s 6d) and to be awarded the Royal Warrant in 2013. It has long had royal connections. Queen Mary's lady in waiting, the Hon Violet d'Arcy, lived at the hotel in 1920; the Norwegian crown prince stayed there for the coronation of George V (he didn't want to share a bath at Buckingham Palace); George VI and the Queen Mother celebrated the end of World War II there with Princess Elizabeth and Princess Margaret (they ate sausages and scrambled eggs) and pastry chefs at the Goring created Prince Charles' christening cake. The family-owned hotel, which is now run by Jeremy Goring, who is the fourth generation of his family to do so, is also a favourite with celebrities: in 1930 novelist Anthony Powell invented the heroine of his novels A Dance to the Music of Time (the Hon Angela Goring) over tea at the hotel, and in 1960 model Jean Shrimpton caused consternation when she wore a mini skirt at its 50th birthday party. Its dining room was designed by the Queen's nephew David Linley.

Top: The Dorchester in the heart of London. Above: The Goring where Kate spent her final night as a single woman, along with her parents and siblings.

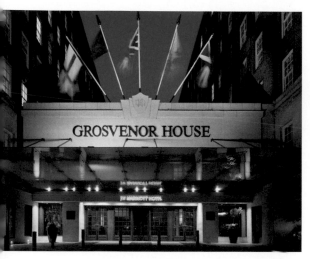

Grosvenor House, 86-90 Park Lane, London W1K 7TN

Prince William disappointed waiting fans when he slipped into the Grosvenor House hotel through a side door to attend rugby player Brian O'Driscoll's 2013 testimonial dinner. He was one of 2,000 guests at the dinner, which honoured the player, who has had the most caps in rugby union history. William, who attended the event in a private capacity, was less shy when he attended UEFA's 37th annual conference of European football's governing body during the 150th anniversary year of the Football Association. The prince, who is patron of the FA, met UEFA President Michael Platini, FIFA President Sepp Blatter and FA Chairman David Bernstein before delivering a speech to welcome London's staging of the Champions League final. Declaring himself 'first and foremost' a football fan, he said: 'It is a great honour for us, the English FA, to host not just this prestigious congress, but of course - the real excitement - tomorrow's Champions League final. My money is on Bayern Munich and two-nil. To host these events during our 150th anniversary year is truly special.' The Grosvenor House hotel, which has the biggest ballroom in London, was originally opened in 1929 with an ice rink in its Great Room - the future Edward VIII attended its Hallowe'en Ice Festival and Dance with the Queen of Spain (a large painting of him is on display in the hotel) and the Queen took ice skating lessons there. In 1934 the Great Room was converted into a ballroom and banqueting space for up to 2,000 people in time for the first Antique Dealers' Fair. The hotel has hosted a variety of newsworthy events including a reception, in 1930, for Amy Johnson, after she became the first woman to fly solo to Australia, and a concert by the Beatles.

Royal Garden Hotel, 2-24 Kensington High Street, London W8 4PT

The Royal Garden Hotel was the location for the Duchess of Cambridge's first official engagement after she announced that she was pregnant with her second child. She and Prince William welcomed Singapore's President Tan and his wife Mary to Britain for their 2014 four-day state visit. The hotel, which boasts panoramic views of Kensington Palace and Hyde Park, opened in 1965 and is the international sportsmen's hotel of choice. It was the official hotel for the FIFA World Cup in 1966, hosted the EUFA Euro '96 Championships, the 1999 Cricket World Cup and the ICC Champions Trophy in 2004 and 2013 and has hosted the 2011 Rugby World Cup winners, the New Zealand All Blacks and the 2007 Cricket Cup winners, Australia. The hotel also boasts a rock star clientele – its 1960s guests include Sonny and Cher, Abba and the Monkees, while contemporary visitors include Rihanna and Justin Bieber.

Top: Grosvenor House boasts a spectacular ball room. Left: William and Kate at the Royal Garden Hotel.

Lancaster Hotel, Lancaster Terrace, London W2 2TY

The Duchess of Cambridge became involved with the Starlight Foundation – the first charity she publicly supported - after attending the 2008 Boodles Boxing Ball at the Lancaster Hotel. She and Prince William watched four old Etonians trade punches with Cambridge graduates to raise money for the charity, set up by former Dynasty actress Emma Samms to grant the wishes of terminally ill children. The couple met Prince Harry and then-girlfriend Chelsy Davey for a champagne reception, dinner and auction, before joining Guy Pelly, Thomas van Straubenzee, Jamie Murray Wells and Jecca Craig in ringside seats for the boxing. The first match featured Jecca's boyfriend Hugh 'The Hitman' Crossley, who lost out to Bear 'The Pain' Maclean. The group then watched William's former classmate James 'The Badger' Meade, son of the international show jumper Richard Meade, being beaten by Al 'Bonecrusher' Poulain, a former equerry to Prince Charles. Kate winced and covered her eyes during the fights, while William and Harry punched the air, showing their Help for Heroes wristbands. The £100-a-ticket event was organised by their friend Charlie Gilkes, who owned Kitts nightclub (now closed). As well as raising £120,000 for the charity, it fulfilled the wish of cystic fibrosis sufferer Bianca Nicholas, 19, to sing for royalty. Kate was so touched by her encounter with Bianca that she suggested forging a link between her family's firm Party Pieces, and the Foundation.

The Savoy, Savoy Way, London WC2R 0EU

Prince William did a double take when he walked into a charity dinner at The Savoy hotel and spotted a cake shaped like his Aston Martin wedding car. William was attending a fundraiser, hosted by the October Club, in aid of the charity St Giles' Trust, which aims to stop criminals reoffending, when he saw the car complete with himself and his wife (only the windscreen, Kate's veil and the balloon wires were not edible). The cake, donated to the charity by baker Claudia Newberry, of Purple Flour, was being auctioned to raise money for the charity, of which William is patron. 'This charity truly inspires me, he said. 'It has touched the lives of a quarter of a million people over the past five decades. What started as a small soup kitchen for the homeless and destitute has become one of the leading charities in this country helping ex-offenders to reform, resettle, and – critically- to break out of the costly and destructive cycle of reoffending.' The Savoy hotel lies on a stretch of land between the Strand and the River Thames, which was once the home of the Count of Savoy – he was given the land by Henry III in 1246 and built his Savoy Palace there. Six hundred years later, in 1881, impresario Richard D'Oyly Carte, chose the site to open his new Savoy Theatre, where he staged his Gilbert and Sullivan operettas. Eight years later, he built next-door to the theatre, The Savoy hotel – the first in London to be lit by electricity, have 'ascending rooms' (lifts) and 'speaking tubes'. Chef Auguste Escoffier created Melba toast for Dame Nellie Melba (when she was on a diet) and Pêches Melba (when she was not); artists Whistler and Monet painted views from The Savoy windows and Oscar Wilde stayed with his friend Lord Alfred Douglas. The actress Vivien Leigh met her first husband Sir Laurence Olivier at the hotel; Winston Churchill frequently lunched there with his cabinet during World War II and the Queen was first seen with the Duke of Edinburgh in public at a Savoy reception.

Top: the Lancaster Hotel.
Above: The Savoy.

MUSEUMS & GALLERIES

Dulwich Picture Gallery, Gallery Road, London SE21 7AD

Above: Kate watches a young artist at work. Above right: Kate shares a laugh with her father-in-law Prince Charles as they create self-portraits.

With a shared love of the arts, it was only a matter of time until the Prince of Wales took his wife and daughter-in-law to an art gallery – but he did not expect to end up doing the ironing. In their first joint engagement, in 2012, the trio visited the Dulwich Picture Gallery where Charles introduced Kate to his Foundation for Children & the Arts. The royals met children taking part in the Great Art Quest, which introduces children to local galleries, professional artists and storytellers, and talked to them about its Face Britain, a project in which their self-portraits were being combined into a montage and beamed onto the front of Buckingham Palace for the Queen's Diamond Jubilee celebrations. They then took part in a class making collage self-portraits, ironing their designs onto silk. 'I don't think I put on eyebrows,' Charles laughed, wielding an iron. 'Do I keep ironing that? I'm going to be here all afternoon.' Asked later if it was the first time Charles had done the ironing, Camilla said with a smile: 'I've got him well-trained with an iron.' Founded in 1811 when Royal Academician Sir Francis Bourgeois bequeathed his collection of old masters to Dulwich College, (stipulating that they should be exhibited publicly) and designed by Sir John Soane, Dulwich Picture Gallery is the first-purpose built public art gallery in the world. Bourgeois built up the collection (with Frenchman Noël Desenfans, who died before him) after being commissioned by Stanislaus Augustus, King of Poland, to form a Royal Collection from scratch, but was left with the collection when the king was forced to abdicate. Since then many celebrated artists have visited the gallery including Monet and Van Gogh.

Imperial War Museum, Lambeth Road, London SE1 6HZ

With his military background, Prince William was the ideal person to launch the Imperial War Museum's fundraising campaign to create a gallery to mark the centenary of World War I. The royal patron of the First World War Galleries: Centenary Campaign, attended a reception with his wife, in 2012 to raise money for the charitable trust. He and Kate were then shown the plans for the galleries. Two years later, William returned with Prime Minister David Cameron to open the galleries and placed the gloves of Major James McCudden on display in the 'Machines Against Men' exhibit. (Major McCudden was awarded the Victoria Cross, after being shot down by more than five enemy planes.) Speaking at the event, William said: 'These Galleries bring to life the common effort and common sacrifices of those who lived through the First World War. Today, I am proud to declare them officially open. In 1920, King George V believed this museum would be an inspiration for future generations. I am very pleased to say it is.' The Imperial War Museum was established before the end of World War I to ensure that future generations remembered the toil and sacrifice of that generation. It underwent a £40 million transformation before the centenary of the war, building the new galleries and atrium. They have also launched a digital collection of records to commemorate all those who served in the war.

Madame Tussauds, Marylebone Road, London NW1 5LR

Visitors to Madame Tussauds can see two life-size wax figures of the Duke and Duchess of Cambridge. The couple was originally modelled in the outfits they wore for their engagement photograph but the waxwork is now clothed in evening dress – William is wearing black tie while Kate is dressed in a turquoise dress by Issa, who was once one of her favourite designers. William and Kate's waxworks stand in the museum's Royal zone with the Queen and Prince Philip, Prince Charles and Camilla, Prince Harry and the late Princess Diana. The museum also has replicas of former monarchs Henry VIII and Elizabeth I. Madame Tussauds Studios have been making wax figures for more than 150 years and now has attractions around the world. A team of 20 sculptors works for four months on each waxwork, using 500 precise body measurements, inserting real hairs (one by one) and countless layers of paint to achieve the correct tint.

Above: Kate at the Imperial War Museum.
Left: waxworks of William and Kate at Madame Tussauds.

National Maritime Museum, Park Row, London SE10 9NF

As a keen sailor, the Duchess of Cambridge was the ideal choice to join Sir Ben Ainslie at a breakfast reception at the National Maritime Museum to launch Britain's bid to win the 2017 America's Cup (or Auld Mug as it is affectionately known), the oldest trophy in sport. The cup, which was made by the jeweller Garrard, was first offered as a prize by Queen Victoria in 1851 – she volunteered to present it to the winner of a sailing race around the Isle of Wight – and was renamed after the New York schooner America won the first race. Britain has yet to win the competition but sponsors such as Simon Le Bon (the Duran Duran star is a keen sailing enthusiast), hope to reverse its fortune. Owned by Royal Museums Greenwich, the National Maritime Museum is set in the Maritime Greenwich World Heritage Site, which encompasses the town centre, Royal Park, Royal Observatory and 17th century Queen's House, which was designed by Inigo Jones and was the first Palladian building in England. The Museum buildings began life in 1807 as a school for the children of seafarers. It was opened to the public by George VI in 1937. The Duchess of Cambridge has also visited Greenwich Park, during the 2012 London Olympics. She joined the royal family watching Zara help Britain secure a silver medal in the team equestrian event.

Top: Kate attends a breakfast reception at the National Maritime Museum in Greenwich to launch Britain's bid for the America's cup. Above: Kate with Sir Ben Ainslie at the National Maritime Museum.

National Portrait Gallery, St. Martin's Place, London WC2H 0HE

The Duchess of Cambridge has a lifelong passion for art – she was a student at the British Institute in Florence in her gap year, gained a 2:1 degree in History of Art from St Andrews University, and made her first solo public visit to the National Portrait Gallery. Kate, who is patron of the gallery, was given a personal tour of the Lucien Freud Portraits exhibition in 2012 by gallery director Sandy Nairne. Five months later, she returned to the gallery, to launch its Olympics exhibition (she wore a £49,000 gold Cartier necklace which echoed the Olympic logo). She looked around the exhibition Road to 2012: Aiming High, which included a black and white photograph of the Duchess playing hockey at the Olympic Park. The next time Kate went to the gallery was in 2012 to unveil her first official portrait, painted by artist Paul Elmsley (the Duchess had two sittings at the artist's studio in the West Country). Since then she has hosted a reception for the charity The Art Room, attended a Portrait Gala dinner (where she was introduced to transvestite potter Grayson Perry, who joked that 'the girl wearing rocks had met the guy wearing frocks') and launched a campaign to save a £12.5 million Van Dyck self-portrait for the nation (the only portrait of the artist made during his time in Britain). The National Portrait Gallery was formally established in 1856. Its first portrait, known as the Chandos portrait, was of William Shakespeare. Originally its trustees insisted that 'no portrait of any person still living, or deceased less that ten years, shall be admitted by purchase, donation, or bequest, except only in the case of the reigning Sovereign, and of his or her Consort'. That rule changed in 1969 – hence the portrait of Kate.

Natural History Museum, Cromwell Road, London SW7 5BD

The first time that the Duchess of Cambridge visited the Natural History Museum was as a schoolgirl – she did not return until 20 years later when she walked through its doors as the wife of Prince William and patron of the museum. It was in 2012 that Kate returned to the gallery to launch the museum's Treasures Gallery, a collection of 22 of its most exceptional exhibits, drawn from an archive of 80 million species and artefacts (her favourite was a copy of the world's most expensive book John James Audubon's Birds of America). 'William and I are just two of millions of people who have passed through these doors and marvelled at the wonders of the natural world, housed in this beautiful gallery,' she said. The following year Kate returned with her husband to attend the premiere of a Sir David Attenborough film 'Natural History Museum Alive 3D' and in 2014 the couple took Prince George to see its Sensational Butterflies exhibition (the moment when Prince George tottered among the butterflies was captured by photographer John Stillwell and released on his 1st birthday). Kate also attended the black-tie Wildlife Photographer of the Year Awards. The Natural History Museum began life as a department of the British Museum, which housed the collection of Sir Hans Sloane, an 18th century physician and collector, who offered his specimens to the Crown for £20,000, payable to his two surviving daughters. It moved to its current site in 1881, merging with the Geological Museum a century later, and now has more than 80 million insects, plants, animals, fossils, rocks and minerals from around the world. Behind the scenes its scientists research world problems such as disease, climate change and threats to the Earth's biodiversity.

Top: Kate waves to well wishers as she attends the National Portrait Gallery. Above: the Natural History Museum.

Royal Academy, Burlington House, Piccadilly, London W1J 0BD

The Duchess of Cambridge flew the flag for Great Britain when she attended a 2012 cocktail party at the Royal Academy to celebrate all things British. Kate walked down the red carpet to the Creative Industries reception and was greeted by David Cameron (it was the first time the Duchess had been photographed with the Prime Minister). Opening the event, he revealed a conversation he had enjoyed with Prince William at the opening ceremony of the Olympic Games. Turning to Kate, he said: 'My favourite part of the opening ceremony was when your husband leant over and said to me: "I don't know if you know, Prime Minister, but my grandmother is a great fan of Dizzee Rascal."' The comment prompted howls of laughter from guests as the rapper, known for hits such as Bonkers, was an unlikely favourite of the Queen. The event, which was attended by 800 guests, including Lily Cole, Stella McCartney, Sir Terence Conran, Roger Daltry, Arlene Phillips and Lulu, was thrown by The Founders Forum to celebrate British culture, creativity, art and entertainment, on the back of the Government's GREAT initiative. The Founders Forum was set up by Jonnie Goodwin and Brent Hoberman of lastminute.com as a community for the best global entrepreneurs in the areas of media and technology. It brings together more than 1,000 of the world's most influential business people. The Royal Academy of Arts, which is based in Burlington House, was founded in 1768 by George III to promote British design. It is known for its Summer Exhibition.

The Royal Society, 6-9 Carlton House Terrace, London SW1Y 5AG

The Duke and Duchess of Cambridge made their first official appearance after becoming parents in 2013 when they attended the inaugural Tusk Conservation Awards. The couple livened up the world's oldest scientific academy, when they turned up for the ceremony, which recognised outstanding figures in African conservation. 'This is our first evening out without him,' said William, referring to Prince George. 'Please excuse us if you see us nervously casting surreptitious glances at mobiles.' William, who is patron of Tusk, presented two awards: a lifetime achievement honour called The Prince William Award for Conservation in Africa, to Clive Stockil, who works at the Lowveld Rhino Trust, in Zimbabwe, and the Tusk Award for Conservation to an up-and-coming award for Kenyan Tom Lalampaa. 'Catherine and I very much hope to introduce George to east Africa – a place we know and love – in the fullness of time," William added. The Royal Society is a Fellowship of the world's most eminent scientists from the worlds of science, engineering and medicine. Founded in 1660, it is the oldest scientific academy in continuous existence.

Above: the Royal Academy. Left: William and Kate make their first official appearance after becoming parents at the inaugural Tusk Conservation Awards.

Saatchi Gallery, Duke Of York's HQ, The Duke Of York Square, King's Road, London SW3 4RY

The Duke and Duchess of Cambridge wandered around modern works of art at the Saatchi Gallery when they attended the 2009 Starlight Foundation Ball. Kate first became involved with the charity, set up by former Dynasty star Emma Samms, to fulfill the wishes of terminally ill children, the previous year, after meeting cystic fibrosis sufferer Bianca Nicholas at the Boodles Boxing Ball. She then agreed to become chairwoman of its fundraiser and joined the Middleton clan at the ball, held in the contemporary art gallery. The gallery, which aims to promote unknown artists, was opened by former advertising legend Charles Saatchi more than 25 years ago – he was the man who discovered Damien Hirst and Tracey Emin.

Sladmore Contemporary Art Gallery, 32 Bruton Place, London W1J 6NW

Prince William spoke for the first time about the devastating loss of losing his mother as a teenager when he met bereaved families during a 2009 charity launch at the Sladmore Contemporary Art Gallery. The prince publicly announced his patronage of the Child Bereavement charity, during its launch of its 'Remember on Mother's Day' campaign. Following in the footsteps of his own mother Princess Diana, who was a close friend of the charity's founding patron Julia Samuel, he said: 'What my mother recognised then – and what I understand now – is that losing a close family member is one of the hardest experiences that anyone can ever endure. I can therefore wholeheartedly relate to the Mother's Day campaign as I too have felt – and still feel – the emptiness on such a day as Mother's Day. It is so painful for grieving families: for mothers remembering a lost child or for children longing for their mother – a day of happiness turned to sadness.' Afterwards he added: 'Never being able to say the word "Mummy" again in your life sounds like a small thing. However for many, including me, it's not really just a word – hollow and evoking only memories.' Child Bereavement UK was set up to provide support for bereaved children and their families. Its Mother's Day campaign was designed to encourage people to spare a thought for mothers who have lost a child or children who have lost their mothers. The Sladmore Contemporary Art Gallery was founded in 1965 and specialises in fine bronze sculptures. Its Jermyn Street gallery displays work by famous artists such as Auguste Rodin, Aristide Maillol, Edgar Degas, Rembrandt Bugatti and Antoine-Louis Barye while its Bruton Place Gallery carries sculptures by contemporary artists.

Top: the Saatchi Gallery. Above: William at the Sladmore Contemporary Art Gallery with Child Bereavement UK's founding patron Julia Samuel.

V&A Museum of Childhood, Cambridge Heath Road, London E2 9PA

The Duchess of Cambridge was preparing for motherhood - before she got pregnant with Prince George - when she paid a secret solo visit to the V&A Museum of Childhood. Kate was given a guided tour of the museum and looked around its exhibition The Stuff of Nightmares, which explored the darker side of traditional fairy tales. The gallery was transformed into a forest for the exhibition (the installation made by local schoolchildren working with artists) for the re-telling of the Brothers Grimm's fairy tale Fundevogel and included a police 'identity parade' of villainous toy suspects. The V&A Museum in Bethnal Green, which was designed by James William Wild as an extension of the main museum, was opened by the future Edward VII in 1872 (Wild had originally designed a garden, clock tower and library but, due to lack of funds, his design was only fully realised in the 1871 edition of The Builder magazine). Intended to be educational, female inmates of Woking Gaol laid the fish-scale patterned marble floor while female students from the V&A's Mosaic Class helped create some of the murals. During the 20th century, head curator Arthur Sabin began to make the museum more child-friendly, setting up a classroom, employing teachers and sourcing toys. He was helped in his endeavours by George V's wife Queen Mary, who donated many toys of her own. But it was not until 1974, after Sir Roy Strong became director of the V&A and instigated changes, that the museum became dedicated to childhood.

London Zoo, Regent's Park, London NW1 4RY

Prince William had a day out with his father at London Zoo in 2013 when they held their first official meeting with wildlife conservationists. The princes launched their 'United for Wildlife' initiative, in the new Tiger Territory at the zoo. There they met two five-year-old Sumatran tigers, a male called Jae Jae, and his mate Melati, who face an uncertain future in the wild. The keepers left nothing to chance, plying them with fresh horse meat and spraying their enclosures with perfume which stimulates their scent marking instincts (Jae Jae prefers Old Spice while Melati is partial Jo Malone). Keeper Teague Stubbington said: 'We have kept back a little of their breakfast - horse meat today - in order to encourage them out of their enclosures. This is quite normal and helps to stimulate their natural hunting behaviour. We will often hide it and make a game of finding it. I have also been leaving a trail of perfume - Hugo Boss today. Tigers don't hide away in the jungle, they like to advertise their presence. Putting perfume down helps to stimulate their scent marking behaviour.' United for Wildlife, of which William is president, is an umbrella body which encompasses seven of the world's biggest campaigners including WWF-UK and the Zoological Society of London (ZSL). Founded in 1826, the Zoological Society of London (ZSL) is an international scientific, conservation and educational charity, which aims to conserve animals and their habitats worldwide.

Top: the V&A Museum of Childhood with its exterior designed by James William Wild. Above: William and Charles tour the Tiger Territory at London Zoo.

PATRONAGES

Centrepoint, 59 Greek Street Street, London W1D 4DH

Prince William cooked breakfast for the homeless at a hostel in Greek Street after sleeping rough on the streets of London (on a piece of cardboard, in a sleeping bag). The prince, who is patron of the charity Centrepoint, spent the night, in the run-up to Christmas 2009, lying in an alleyway, surrounded by wheelie bins, in order to highlight the plight of the homeless. But he was slightly better off than the other rough sleepers at Blackfriars Bridge as he was not alone (he was accompanied by an armed police protection officer, his private secretary Jamie Lowther-Pinkerton, a former SAS officer, and the chief executive of the charity, Seyi Obakin). Afterwards he went back to Centrepoint's hostel where he showered, before cooking breakfast and cutting a cake to celebrate the charity's 40th anniversary. Later he joined the Queen for her traditional Christmas lunch at Buckingham Palace. 'I cannot, after one night, even begin to imagine what it must be like to sleep rough on London's streets night after night', he said. 'I hope that by deepening my understanding of the issue, I can do my bit to help the most vulnerable on our streets.' Since William's visit the hostel has closed. It was decommissioned by Westminster Council in 2014 because of the age of the building.

Hope House, 52 Rectory Grove, London SW4 0EB

The Duchess of Cambridge showed off her baby bump for the first time in public in 2013 when she visited a residential centre for women, who had an addiction to drink, drugs or gambling. Kate chatted to women in an art therapy class at the Grade II* listed Hope House, near Clapham Common, which is run by the charity Action on Addiction. 'Well done for getting sober,' she said. It was the second time that Kate, who is patron of the charity, had visited the centre (she made a private visit in 2011 before announcing her patronage). Her visit coincided with the announcement that Action on Addiction would be the first charity to receive funds raised by 100 Women in Hedge Funds. In a letter, released to mark the launch, she wrote: 'Those affected by addiction are in desperate need of the highest level of care and treatment. Whether direct or indirect, the impact of addiction can be devastating.'

Top: William cuts the cake at the 40th anniversary of the charity Centrepoint. Left: Kate chats to children at Clapham's Grade II* listed Hope House.

Only Connect, York House, 207 – 221 Pentonville Road, London, N1 9UZ

The Duke and Duchess of Cambridge struggled to keep their composure on a visit to the crime prevention charity Only Connect after a male dancer began twerking during a contemporary dance performance. The couple arrived arm in arm at the HQ of the charity, in King's Cross, and met some of the 10,000 ex-offenders and young people at risk of offending that it supports each year. The couple also met workers at the charity Handmade Alliance, one of a group of charities, based in the 'enterprise hub' at King's Cross, which employs ex-offenders to make textiles for British designers.

St Giles Trust, Georgian House, 64-68 Camberwell Church Street, London SE5 8JB

Prince William praised the 'remarkable strength of character' of ex-offenders trying to find jobs when he made a solo visit to the HQ of the St Giles Trust. There he met team leader Junior Smart, who had turned his life around after serving a drugs sentence and now works with serving prisoners. 'I think a lot of employers don't understand from where a lot of ex-offenders come,' said William, 'the lessons they've learnt just from being in prison or being at rock bottom. I think it shows remarkable strength of character. That in itself is a quality that should be put forward to the employers.' St Giles Trust trains reformed ex-offenders to help other offenders turn their lives around, helping them find somewhere to live and something to live for and giving them support.

Shooting Star House Children's Hospice, The Avenue, Hampton TW12 3RA

The Duchess of Cambridge won over a five-year-old girl when she visited the hospice where she was recovering from a kidney transplant – and was given a hug and a thumbs up. Kate, who is patron of East Anglia's Children's Hospices, met Demi-Leigh Armstrong when she toured the Shooting Star House Children's Hospice in 2013 and joined a music therapy session. After coaxing some of the children to sing with a frog puppet, she offered Demi-Leigh a rattle for her friend, who did not have a musical instrument. But Demi-Leigh turned her back on the Duchess after saying: 'No." It was only when Kate went to leave the hospice, that Demi-Leigh grabbed her leg and said: 'Give me a hug first.' She then had a cuddle with the future Queen and gave a thumbs-up. Shooting Star House is run by the charity Shooting Star Chase, caring for babies, children and young people, who have life-limiting conditions, and their families. They offer support at their two hospices, Shooting Star House, in Hampton, and Christopher's in Guildford.

Above: William and Kate at Only Connect.
Left: Kate coaxes youngsters to sing using a frog puppet.

PUBS & RESTAURANTS

L'Anima, 1 Snowden Street, London EC2A 2DQ

This southern Italian restaurant was the venue for a 2014 Autumn Gala organised by the charity Action on Addiction. During a champagne reception, the Duchess of Cambridge, who is patron of the charity, met supporters including the disgraced tycoon Hans Rausing (he kept his wife Eva's body in the house for two months after she died from a drug overdose). Kate had dinner and watched a stand-up routine by impersonator Rory Bremner. L'Anima (Italian for 'the soul') is an award-winning Italian restaurant in the heart of the City. Its chef is Francesco Mazzei, who is inspired by his childhood in Calabria, and has worked at restaurants such as The Dorchester, Rome's Eden Terrazza and Edinburgh's Santini.

The Bluebird, 350 King's Road, London SW3 5UU

The Duchess and Duchess of Cambridge were often spotted dining at The Bluebird restaurant when they were dating – it was not far from her bachelor pad in Chelsea. Housed in the former Bluebird Garage, the Conran restaurant serves classic British cuisine under head chef Matthew Robinson. The Grade II* listed art deco building, was built in 1923 for the Bluebird Motor Company (at the time its garages were the largest in Europe), which was connected to land speed record breaker Malcolm Campbell, but folded in 1927. It later became an ambulance station and fashion market before being converted by Sir Terence Conran in 1997 into a restaurant, bar, café and supermarket (as well as The Shop at Bluebird).

Builders Arms, 13 Britten Street, London SW3 3TY

When the Duchess of Cambridge lived in Chelsea she would often enjoy a leisurely Sunday lunch with Prince William at the gastro-pub The Builders Arms. A short stroll down the King's Road from her flat, the pub lies in the shadow of St Luke's Church. It may be hard to find but it is worth the effort. Voted 12th best pub in the UK in the 2004 Morning Advertiser Pub Awards, it is a favourite with locals and people in the know.

Top: the southern Italian restaurant L'Anima. Middle: The Bluebird, close to Kate's former bachelor pad. Bottom: Kate's old local, the Builders Arms.

Bumpkin, 209 Westbourne Park Road, London W11 1EA

The Duke and Duchess of Cambridge chose Bumpkin, in Notting Hill, for their 2012 staff Christmas party. They hired the Queen's Room (named after its portrait of the sovereign) and laid on a £30 traditional menu of turkey and Christmas pudding. A stone's throw from Portobello Road, the restaurant is one of four Bumpkin brasseries in London which serve locally-sourced seasonal British dishes.

The Collection, 264 Brompton Road, London SW3 2AS

The Duke and Duchess of Cambridge enjoyed one of their final carefree nights as students after leaving St Andrews in the summer of 2005 at The Collection, a bar and restaurant, housed in an old warehouse in Chelsea's fashionable Brompton Triangle, which was a favourite haunt for celebrities. The building had previously been home to a Porsche garage, a Conran furniture shop and a Katharine Hamnett boutique, and was renowned for its entrance – an 80ft catwalk, designed by the architect Sir Norman Foster – and its long bar. (It has recently been redesigned by Tom Dixon.) After having a few drinks – William stuck to red wine while Kate sipped margaritas – it was on to the nightclub Purple, which has since closed. The couple, for once, let their hair down. After spending some time in the VIP room, they took to the dance floor, where William drank sambuca, chatted with the DJ and requested a few tracks for his girlfriend, including Shakedown by rapper DMX, dance hit I Like the Way you Move by BodyRockers and Starsailor's Four to the Floor. They finally emerged at 1.30 a.m. looking slightly the worse for wear.

Dans Le Noir, 30-31 Clerkenwell Green, London EC1R 0DU

The Duke and Duchess of Cambridge are rumoured to have enjoyed romantic suppers at Dans Le Noir before they married. Certainly it is the ideal venue for people who want to remain anonymous – dinner is served in complete darkness by blind waiters. Located in Clerkenwell, Dans Le Noir can serve 60 people in its 'dark room'. It also has a lit bar and private lounge.

Top: Bumpkin, where Kate and William held their staff Christmas party. Middle: The Collection. Left: Kate and William allegedly enjoyed romantic suppers at Dans Le Noir.

The Hambrough Tavern, The Broadway, Southall UB1 1NG

This pub was the venue of the wedding reception of Kate's grandparents Ronald and Dorothy Goldsmith in the Queen's Coronation year. The pub later became notorious as a haunt of racist skinheads – it was burned down during an 1981 gig by Asian youths, who were rioting over the death of teacher Blair Peach during clashes between police and anti-fascist demonstrations.

The Troubadour Café, 265 Old Brompton Road, London SW5 9JA

Princes William and Harry were the guests of honour at The Troubadour Café in 2009 when they attended the launch of the Henry van Straubenzee Memorial Fund. The princes, who are joint patrons of the charity, were close friends of Henry, who was killed in a car crash at the age of 18, and his older brother Thomas, when they were at Ludgrove prep school. Established in 1954, the Troubadour is one of the last remaining coffee houses of its era. Its club room in the cellar was renowned as being one of the primary venues of the British folk revival in the 1950s and 1960s.

Above: Kate's grandparents at their wedding reception at The Hambrough Tavern. Left: the coffee house, The Troubadour Café.

ROYAL RESIDENCES

Buckingham Palace, London SW1A 1AA

The Duke and Duchess of Cambridge held their 2011 wedding reception at Buckingham Palace – they kissed twice on the balcony – and spent their first night as man and wife in its Belgian Suite, traditionally reserved for heads of state. The couple travelled in an open-topped carriage for the 15-minute journey from Westminster Abbey to Buckingham Palace, while, in a surprise gift for the groom, who was an RAF search and rescue helicopter pilot, a yellow Sea King rescue helicopter joined them on the route down The Mall. The Queen then hosted a canapé reception for 650 guests at Buckingham Palace. Afterwards the couple looked visibly moved at the fly-past of Lancasters, Spitfires and Hurricanes from the RAF's Battle of Britain Memorial Flight. Finally as the crowd dispersed, Prince William emerged at the wheel of his father's classic blue Aston Martin, which his brother had decked in ribbons and balloons, with a 'JU5T WED' number plate, and drove his bride back to Clarence House. There they changed for the dinner dance, hosted by Prince Charles. During the speeches, Michael Middleton said: 'I knew things were getting serious when I found a helicopter in my garden. I thought: "Gosh. He must like my daughter." I did wonder then how William was going to top this, if they ever got engaged. I just thought: "What will he do?" You can't get much better than that. We are certainly not used to princes landing helicopters in the garden.' The official London residence of the sovereign, Queen Victoria was the first monarch to live at Buckingham Palace. Since then it has hosted both personal and state occasions: state banquets, investitures, garden parties, staff Christmas lunches and glittering receptions. Prince William was the fourth – and last - royal baby to be christened in its Music Room by the Archbishop of Canterbury (as were Prince Charles, Princess Anne and Prince Andrew); Prince Charles celebrated his 60th birthday at the

Above: Buckingham Palace.

palace and Prince George has weekly swimming lessons there. William and Kate undertook their first official duty as a married couple when they greeted President Barack Obama and his wife at the start of their three-day State Visit (Kate eclipsed Michelle in a £175 Reiss dress which promptly sold out); and the Duchess undertook her first joint engagement with the Queen, taking a private tour of the wedding exhibition ('It's made to look very creepy,' was the Queen's verdict on the headless mannequin.) George III bought Buckingham House, as it was known then, in 1761, for his wife Queen Charlotte as a family home and it became known as the 'Queen's House' – 14 of his 15 children were born there. It was transformed into a palace by George IV – its state rooms, designed by architect John Nash, remain virtually unchanged today. Queen Victoria was the first sovereign to live at Buckingham Palace (she left from there for her Coronation). She hired architect Edward Blore to build a fourth wing for her family, creating a quadrangle. Buckingham Palace now has 775 rooms, including 19 state rooms, 52 royal and guest bedrooms, 188 staff bedrooms, 92 offices and 78 bathrooms. The Queen and Duke of Edinburgh live in private apartments on the north side of the palace, while other members of the royal family occupy rooms on the upper floors of the north and east sides – the ground floor and south wing are used by Household staff. The Prime Minister has a weekly audience with the Queen when they are both in London and the Chancellor of the Exchequer has an audience with her before the Budget. The State Rooms are open to visitors each year.

Above: William and Kate's first kiss on the balcony of Buckingham Palace.

Clarence House, Little St James's Street, London SW1A 1BA

Six months after her marriage, the Duchess of Cambridge undertook her first solo engagement at Clarence House when Prince Charles was suddenly forced to travel to Saudi Arabia for the funeral of their crown prince. The Prince of Wales asked his 'darling daughter-in-law' to host the reception and dinner at his London residence for the charity In Kind Direct, which redistributes surplus goods and cash donations from big business to small charities. Kate was a regular visitor to Clarence House before her wedding – William and Harry had an apartment there (she threw a surprise farewell party there in 2006 before William went to Sandhurst). Designed by John Nash, Clarence House was built in 1827 for George III's third son, Prince William Henry, Duke of Clarence and his wife Adelaide (the future William IV). When he succeeded to the throne, he decided to remain there, rather than moving to Buckingham Palace. Prince Charles first lived at Clarence House when he was a toddler - the Queen and the Duke of Edinburgh spent their early married years there and Princess Anne was born there. After she ascended to the throne, the Queen and Prince Philip moved into Buckingham Palace – and Clarence House became the home of the Queen Mother and Princess Margaret. A bon viveur, the Queen Mum hosted lavish luncheons and evening receptions at Clarence House, entertaining all foreign Heads of State for tea on the afternoon of the first day of a State Visit. After her 70th birthday, in 2001, the royal family would assemble at Clarence House each year for her traditional birthday appearance – well wishers would gather in the Stable Yard Road outside Clarence House to offer greetings and presents. After her death, Prince Charles inherited the house and hired interior designer Robert Kime to give it a revamp. It is open to the public during the summer months.

Above: Kate and William announce their engagement. Above right: Clarence House.

57 Clarence Street, Southall UB2 5BJ

This street in Southall, once home to the jazz singer Cleo Laine's parents, boasts one of the Duchess of Cambridge's ancestral homes: her great-grandparents Charlie and Edith Goldsmith lived there during World War I and her grandfather Ronald was born there and lived there until the age of six. Sadly Charlie (nicknamed 'Putty' by his mates) returned from the Great War suffering from emphysema and died in 1938, leaving his widow in penury. She moved to a condemned flat in Dudley Road, a scruffier street, parallel to Clarence Street, which has since been demolished. Southall is now a predominantly Asian area but in those days it was a white working-class suburb, providing labour for the sprawling brick factories, flour mills and chemical plants, the railway depots and engineering works that had sprung up around the Grand Junction Canal (once the main freight route between London and Birmingham), Brunel's Great Western Railway and the Uxbridge Road.

Kensington Palace, Kensington Gardens, London W8 4PX

Top: Kate's grandfather Ronald Goldsmith's sisters Hetty, Ede (carrying Joyce), and Alice, outside 57 Clarence Street. Above: William joins Jon Bon Jovi and Taylor Swift in an impromptu performance of Living On A Prayer during the 2013 Winter Whites Gala in aid of Centrepoint at Kensington Palace.

Once inhabited by Princess Margaret, Apartment 1A, in the clock tower, at Kensington Palace is now the London home of the Duke and Duchess of Cambridge. The couple moved into the 57-room residence after a £5.5 million renovation – Prince George celebrated his first birthday in the apartment in 2014 (guests included the Queen and Michael and Carole Middleton) and the Mothering Sunday photograph of William, Kate, George and Lupo, was taken in the window of their new home. Originally known as Nottingham House, the Jacobean palace was bought by William III from his Secretary of State, the Earl of Nottingham. He commissioned Christopher Wren to extend the house and build the Royal Apartments, Council Chamber, Chapel Royal and Great Stairs. A private road (wide enough for three or four carriages to travel abreast) was laid out from the Palace to Hyde Park Corner (a length survives today as Rotten Row). Kensington Palace was the favourite residence of successive sovereigns until the death of George II in 1760. The birthplace and childhood home of Queen Victoria, it was there that she woke up in her wooden and gilt bateau lit on June 20, 1837, to be told that she was Queen of England. She immediately moved to Buckingham Palace and never stayed in Kensington again. The Queen's grandmother Queen Mary was born in at Kensington in 1867 and the Duke of Edinburgh stayed there in his grandmother's apartment in 1947 between his engagement and marriage to the Queen. William and Kate have hosted a number of events at the Palace including the 2013 Winter Whites Gala in aid of Centrepoint, when William joined Jon Bon Jovi and Taylor Swift in an impromptu performance of Living On A Prayer.

20 Kingsbridge Road, Norwood Green, Southall UB2 5RT

The childhood home of Prince William's mother-in-law, Carole Middleton lived there from the age of 11 until she met husband Michael. Carole's parents Ronald and Dorothy bought the three-bedroom house in 1966, (a year after the birth of their son Gary), for £4,950 – the equivalent of £135,000 today - and stayed there for the next 25 years until their children had grown up and left home.

Old Church Street, London SW3 5DL

Old Church Street has the distinction of being the oldest street in Chelsea and home to the Duchess of Cambridge's bachelor apartment. Her parents Mike and Carole bought the flat for £780,000 in 2002, shortly after she moved in with Prince William, and she lived there after moving up to town when she left university. The street, which is named after its church, Chelsea Old Church, has had a number of famous occupants: 19th century novelist Charles Kingsley (who wrote the Water Babies) lived at number 56; painter Augustus John built number 28 just before World War I; and author AA Milne, who wrote Winnie the Pooh in the 1920's, lived at number 13. During the 1960s, the street was home to the recording studios Sound Techniques (46a), which was where singer-songwriter Nick Drake recorded his first album 'Five Leaves Left' (Pink Floyd and The Who also recorded there). It is now the location of the Chelsea Arts Club and the shoe designer Manolo Blahnik.

St James' Palace, Marlborough Road, London SW1A 1BS

The Duchess of Cambridge first visited St James' Palace in 2008 when she attended the wedding of Prince William's second cousin Lady Rose Windsor, who works in the film industry, and her husband George Gilman, the son of a former director of Leeds United Football Club – she went alone to the ceremony in the Queen's Chapel because William was on exercise. Since then she has returned to the Holbein-painted chapel for her confirmation and for the baptism of Prince George. The Archbishop of Canterbury, Justin Welby made the sign of the cross on George's head with water taken from the River Jordan (in a royal tradition that dates back to the 12th century) and poured into the silver Lily Baptismal Font, commissioned by Queen Victoria and Prince Albert in 1840, which has been used at every royal christening since. An intimate ceremony (the guest list did not include Prince Andrew, Prince Edward or Princess Anne), there were just 23 guests including the Queen (who was wearing a diamond, ruby and sapphire broach given to her on the birth of Prince Charles) and Prince Philip, Charles and Camilla, the Middleton family and the seven godparents (Oliver Baker, Emilia Jardine-Paterson, Zara Tindall, William van Cutsem, Hugh, Earl Grosvenor, Jamie Lowther-Pinkerton, and Julia Samuel). Two hymns were chosen by the couple - Breathe on Me, Breath of God and be Thou

Top: 20 Kingsbridge Road. Middle: Old Church Street, the location of Kate's bachelor pad. Left: St James' Palace.

My Vision - while lessons were read by Pippa Middleton (St Luke ch 18, verses 15-17) and Prince Harry (St John ch 15, verses 1-5). Afterwards there was just enough time for tea and a slice of christening cake (in line with tradition, a tier of the couple's wedding cake from 2011) at Clarence House. Photographs of the christening showed - for the first time in more than a century – the monarch with three living heirs: Prince Charles, Prince William and George. The last occasion such a picture was taken was in 1894 when Queen Victoria was photographed with her son Edward VII, grandson George V and great-grandson Edward VIII. St James' Palace, which is not open to the public, has been the setting for some of the most important events in royal history. Built in the 16th century by Henry VIII (its Tudor gatehouse still bears his royal cypher HR), it has been home to a succession of royals including his illegitimate son Henry Fitzroy; his second wife, Anne Boleyn, who stayed there the night after her coronation; and their daughter Elizabeth I. Both Charles II and James II were born and baptised at St James' as were Mary II, Queen Anne and James Stuart (the Old Pretender). After the destruction of the Palace of Whitehall, St James' Palace became the residence of all monarchs until William IV – on his death court functions were still held in the state apartments and Queen Victoria and Prince Albert were married there.

Worcester House, Beaufort Buildings, The Strand, London WC2R 0ET

Before the Duchess of Cambridge, the last commoner to marry a future king was lady's maid Anne Hyde. She married James Duke of York – on September 3, 1660, in a secret wedding ceremony at Worcester House, a mansion on The Strand, which overlooked the River Thames. Performed during the night by the Duke's chaplain at her father's home, Worcester House, and witnessed by only two people, the marriage of the future king James II and his heavily pregnant 23-year-old mistress scandalised the royal court, which could not accept that a blue blood had married a commoner. Since then times have changed and the Duchess of Cambridge has been welcomed into the royal family. Next to The Savoy hotel, Worcester House was owned by the second Marquis of Worcester, father of the first Duke of Beaufort, but was rented for £500 a year by Anne Hyde's father, Lord Clarendon, when the wedding occurred. Samuel Pepys mentions the house in his diaries: 'Here I staid and saw my Lord Chancellor come into his great Hall, where wonderful how much company there was to expect him at a Seale.' The building was eventually demolished by the Duke of Beaufort, who built the Beaufort Buildings on its site (author Henry Fielding lived there in the 18th century).

Above: Royal Guards at St James' Palace.

SCHOOLS

Bacon's College, Timber Pond Road, London SE16 6AT

The Duke and Duchess of Cambridge displayed their sporting prowess – or lack of it - when they visited a college in Rotherhithe. While Kate lost a table tennis game to 13-year-old Hiba Feredj 8-2, William made two attempts to score a goal after running through a series of plastic cones before being passed the ball. He put the first shot 6ft wide and the second over the bar (he later blamed his brown suede shoes). 'Watching me on the football field is never a pretty sight,' he said. 'The expression "giraffe on ice" comes to mind. It's marginally better than to see my brother cheat his way to become the fastest man on the planet,' he joked, referring to Harry's race against Usain Bolt during his tour of the Caribbean. He then praised his wife saying: 'Catherine with a hockey stick is something to behold — and be aware of.' The couple was at Bacon's College launching a pilot scheme run by the Greenhouse charity – and funded by The Royal Foundation - to turn 25 disadvantaged teenagers into the sports coaches of the future.

Blessed Sacrament Roman Catholic Primary School, Boadicea Street, London N1 0UF

The Duchess of Cambridge was reunited with Comic Relief ambassador John Bishop at this primary school in Islington – and he had her in fits of laughter. A year after they launched M-PACT Plus - a collaboration between Comic Relief and the two charities Action on Addiction and Place2Be of which she is patron, in Manchester – the pair visited Blessed Sacrament School to monitor its progress. During a speech, the comedian urged guests not to focus on the 'style icon in their midst' but to focus on the project. 'Basically don't make the story about me,' he joked. Kate burst into giggles and did not stop smiling throughout his speech – when he sat down, she leant over and whispered to him. Kate arrived at the school and made a beeline for the flag-waving children, sinking to her knees and asking them what they liked about school. 'Lunchtime,' one four-year-old quipped, making her smile. Funded by the Royal Foundation and Comic Relief, M-PACT Plus trains school staff to help children affected by their parents' addiction to drugs or alcohol. As Kate left, the pupils presented her with a painting of the Duchess cradling Prince George.

Leiths School of Food and Wine, 16-20 Wendell Road, London W12 9RT

The Duchess of Cambridge did a cookery course at the esteemed Leiths School of Food and Wine before she married Prince William. TV chef Rachel Khoo did a two-week course with Kate, before going on to front her own BBC2 show The Little Paris Kitchen. 'Kate was in my class,' she said. 'She was ill for a few days, so I took notes for her. She was a lovely person, but she kept to herself.'

Top: Bacon's College. Middle: Kate at Blessed Sacrament Roman Catholic Primary School. Left: Leiths School of Food and Wine.

Minors Nursery School, 10 Pembridge Square, London W2 4ED

Prince William made history at the age of three years three months, when he became the first heir to the throne to attend a private nursery school. The prince went to Jane Mynors' nursery school, in a Victorian terraced house, in Chepstow Villas, just five minutes from Kensington Palace – chosen because Princess Diana, who worked as a nursery school helper before her marriage, wanted her son to have a normal education (Prince Charles had a governess at Buckingham Palace). William joined Mrs Mynors' nursery as a 'Cygnet' in 1985, spending a year at the nursery, working his way through the school as a 'Little Swan' until he became a 'Big Swan'. His typical day started with a prayer before he moved onto painting, cutting paper with scissors, singing and playing outdoors (reports suggested at times he was 'a bit of a handful'). William's first role on the stage was as a wolf in his school play 'The Good Little Christmas Tree'. The Minors nursery school is now based in Pembridge Square.

Northolt High School, Vincent Centre, Eastcote Lane, Northolt UB5 4HP

The Duchess of Cambridge was greeted with applause by school pupils in 2014 when she walked into their school hall in Northolt, to officially open their Art Room – built with a £105,000 donation from a charity dealing day at the City firm ICAP. Kate, who is a royal patron of The Art Room, was given a posy by pupils and chatted to children who were attending an art therapy session. At present the Art Room, which organises art therapy for vulnerable children, has 25 other classrooms in schools across London and Oxfordshire. TV presenter Jon Snow, who is another patron, said: 'The Duchess thinks there should be an Art Room in every school in Britain.'

Top: William's first day at Minors Nursery. Right: Kate joins in an art class at Northolt High School.

Old Ford Primary School, Wrights Road, Bow, London E3 5LD

The Duchess of Cambridge surprised a meeting of the new 23rd Poplar Beaver Scout Coloney, in Bow, when she turned up their 2014 Christmas meeting unannounced. Kate, who was wearing a traditional Scout scarf and woggle (the traditional leather fastening) with her favourite J Brand jeans and suede boots, was supporting the Scout Association's 'Better Prepared' campaign. 'Oh my God, it's Princess Kate,' one Scout shouted. The Scouts, who were aged between five and eight years old, were earning their disability awareness badge – Kate giggled as she joined them in trying to ice fairy cakes while blindfolded with her scarf. Afterwards, the Duchess presented each Beaver Scout with their new badge. Scout Association chief commissioner Wayne Bulpitt said: 'We're delighted the Duchess was able to help us.'

Robert Blair Primary School, Brewery Road, London N7 9QJ

The Duchess of Cambridge made a secret visit to an inner city primary school in 2011 to meet children in its Art Room before she announced her patronage of charity. Kate dressed down for the occasion but the pupils, who had mustered in the car park, were unimpressed. 'She doesn't look like a Princess,' one said. 'Where's her dress?' Parents only found out about the VIP visitor when they received a text from the school, which read: 'If your child comes home and says they saw Kate Middleton today, it's true! We had a surprise visit from the Duchess of Cambridge to The Art Room.' The charity, which has 26 Art Rooms in London and Oxfordshire – including that at the Robert Blair school - aims to 'increase self-esteem, self-confidence and independence through art'.

Wetherby Pre-Prep School, 11 Pembridge Square, London W2 4ED

A barrage of photographers greeted Prince William when he turned up for his first day at Wetherby School, a private prep-prep school in Notting Hill, at the age of four, wearing its distinctive grey and red blazer and cap. There William showed a flair for swimming (he was awarded the Grunfield prize for the boy who displayed best overall style) was a regular at school sports' days (Princess Diana memorably took part in the parents' race) and appeared in school concerts. The school, which was founded in 1951, was originally in Wetherby Place – hence the name – but moved to Pembridge Square 20 years later.

Top: Kate helps young scouts at Old Ford Primary School in Bow. Middle: Robert Blair Primary School. Left: William starts at Wetherby Pre-Prep School.

SHOPS

Alexander McQueen, 4-5 Old Bond Street, London W1S 4PD

Sarah Burton became the most famous designer in the world in 2011 when she created the Duchess of Cambridge's wedding dress. A graduate of St Martin's College of Art and Design, she joined Alexander McQueen in 1997 (a year after doing a placement at the company). For 14 years she worked alongside Lee (as he was known to his friends and family), who was her boss, friend and mentor, and when he committed suicide she was heartbroken. After his death, she was appointed head designer and has since won a clutch of awards – she was voted Designer of the Year in 2011, named among Time Magazine's 100 most influential people and awarded an OBE for her services to the British fashion industry.

Alice Temperley, 27 Bruton Street, London W1J 6QN

One of the Duchess of Cambridge's favourite designers, Alice Temperley was the woman who created Pippa Middleton's emerald gown for the evening party at the royal wedding. Kate's sister wore the label Temperley London – a favourite of A-listers such as Rihanna and Gwyneth Paltrow – for the dance in Buckingham Palace's disco-balled Throne Room. (Alice later revealed that they had taken the skylights out of the building for guests to be able to enter across the roof without being seen.) Born in Somerset, the eldest of four children, Alice studied textiles at St Martin's and did a master's degree at the Royal College of Art & Design before setting up her own company in 2001, with husband Lars, a former banker, who is now her business partner. She now has five stores in London and 220 outlets in 35 countries as well as a diffusion line Alice by Temperley.

Asprey, 167 New Bond Street, London W1S 4AY

Society jewellers Asprey was the venue for the Duchess of Cambridge's first appearance in 2007 after she and Prince William split. Kate and Pippa were invited to the launch of author Simon Sebag Montefiore's book Young Sultan at the Bond Street store. There they mingled with guests such as Simon's sister-in-law Tara Palmer-Tomkinson, writers Plum Sykes and William Shawcross, newscaster Emily Maitlis and Conservative MP Nicholas Soames (a friend of Prince Charles). Founded in 1781 by William Asprey, the flagship store in Bond Street opened in 1847. Since then the company has had strong ties with royalty: Queen Victoria awarded the company the Gold Medal at the 1851 Great Exhibition and gave Asprey its first Royal Warrant in 1862 (they have royal warrants from every monarch). In 1925 Queen Mary commissioned Asprey to make a five-strand pearl necklace for Princess Margaret's 18th birthday; in 1973 Ringo Starr was given a bespoke chess set from Asprey as a present; and in 2003 actress Keira Knightley became the new face of Asprey.

Blue Almonds, 164 Walton Street, London SW3 2JL

When the Duchess of Cambridge was spotted shopping in Blue Almonds with her mother Carole, she put the boutique firmly on the map. The £265 Moses basket, which Kate bought for Prince George, flew out of the door. Founded by Polishwoman Izabela Minkiewicz, Blue Almonds first opened its luxury children's boutique in 2007 at 79 Walton Street. It moved to a new location on the other side of the road in 2014 and now has a babies' playing area.

Boomf, 100 Exmouth House, 3-11 Pine Street, London EC1R 0JH

This is the headquarters of Boomf on Demand - the marshmallow company which belongs to the Duchess of Cambridge's brother James Middleton. He set up the mail order company in 2013 and now has a mobile stand in Selfridges, which creates 'edible selfies' by printing Instagram photographs on marshmallows (a box of nine is £12). The on-the-go printing machine is housed in a refurbished 1950s Pashley's ice cream tricycle. When asked who his ideal customer would be, James said: 'I would send it to Willy Wonka and then he would high five me. (This actually happened to me in a dream.)'

Burlington Arcade, 51 Piccadilly, London W1J 0QJ

The Burlington Arcade received a special visitor in 2012 when the Duchess of Cambridge popped into a charity shopping event with her dog Lupo. She was its most high-profile shopper since the arcade was commissioned in 1819 by Lord George Cavendish, who lived in nearby Burlington House (now the Royal Academy) and wanted a covered promenade of shops to stop ruffians throwing rubbish (particularly oyster shells) onto his property. Its first leaseholders – even the male milliners and corsetieres – were addressed as 'Madame'. Burlington Arcade got its first Royal Warrant in 1830 when James Drew was rewarded for making Gladstone's high collars; jeweller Hancocks created the first Victoria Cross in 1856 (they have produced every one of the 1,350 VCs that have been issued); Fred Astaire ordered his velvet slippers there; and Ingrid Bergman made a visit to jewellers Richard Ogden. In 1964, the Arcade witnessed a scene, which could have come from a movie: a Jaguar Mark 10 whizzed down the Arcade and six masked men, armed with axe handles and iron bars, smashed the windows of the Goldsmiths and Silversmiths Association shop stealing £35,000-worth of jewellery. The Arcade has also been the venue for the films Patriot Games, 101 Dalmations and Scandal.

Cath Kidston, French Railways House, 178-180 Piccadilly, London W1J 9ER

Prince George put Cath Kidston on the royal map when he was photographed in a £32 blue tank top, emblazoned with marching guardsmen – it sold out in three weeks. The Yummy Mummy's favourite designer trained with interior designer Nicky Haslam, before opening her first shop in Notting Hill (she spent a third of the £15,000 budget creating a rose print wallpaper). When she made a mistake with an order – she ordered duvet and pillow sets instead of fabric on a roll – she created her first collection. She now has 59 stores.

Fortnum & Mason, 181 Piccadilly, London W1A 1ER

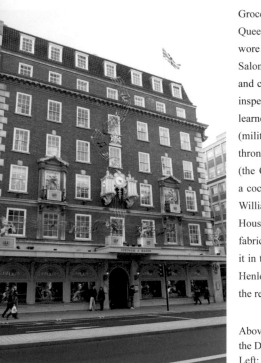

Grocer Fortnum & Mason was the venue for the Duchess of Cambridge's first visit with the Queen and Camilla during the Diamond Jubilee year - and all three generations of the royals wore shades of blue. The trio was in the Piccadilly store to open the Diamond Jubilee Tea Salon (to mark the anniversary Fortnum's sent a United Services Tin of Queen Anne tea and clotted cream digestive biscuits to the 16,000 troops serving abroad). While the Queen inspected the store's honey and preserves and Camilla checked out the bakery section, Kate learned about Fortnum's famous teas. Afterwards they attended a tea party for 150 guests (military personnel and Fortnum's staff, who were on duty when the Queen came to the throne). As a leaving gift, the store gave each of the royals a hamper containing dog biscuits (the Queen is well-known for her corgis, Camilla has three Jack Russells and Kate owns a cocker spaniel called Lupo). Fortnum & Mason was launched in 1707 by royal footman William Fortnum and his landlord Hugh Mason: he sold the leftover wax from the Royal Household, who insisted he lit new candles each night. The store has become part of the fabric of British life – Charles Dickens, Henry James and Wilkie Collins have all mentioned it in their books; Mr Heinz launched his baked bean at Fortnum's, and no visit to Ascot or Henley would be complete without one of their hampers. In 2011, chef Luke Turner entered the record books when he created the world's largest scotch egg (6.955kg).

Above: Kate's first official visit with the Queen and
the Duchess of Cornwall during the Diamond Jubilee.
Left: Fortnum & Mason.

Garrard, 24 Albermarle Street, London W1S 4HT

Garrard has the distinction of being the jeweller who created the royal engagement ring – they made the diamond and sapphire cluster ring for Princess Diana in 1981, and Prince William gave it to Kate in 2010. The royal family's relationship with Garrard began in 1840 when Prince Albert commissioned the company to create a sapphire and white diamond cluster broach as a wedding gift for his future wife, Queen Victoria. Their eldest son, the future Edward VII, followed suit in 1863, ordering a diamond and pearl parure (a set of three matching items) for his future bride, Princess Alexandra. The firm also designed and crafted Queen Mary's 'Fringe Tiara', which the Queen wore on her 1947 wedding day.

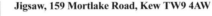

Gieves & Hawkes, 1 Savile Row, London W1S 3JR

Prince William and Prince Harry are the latest male members of the British royal family to be dressed by Savile Row tailors Gieves & Hawkes – they follow in the footsteps of their father Prince Charles, great-grandfather George V and great-great grandfather George VI. Royal warrant holders since 1798, James Gieve and Thomas Hawkes, who were respectively naval and army tailors, supplied the uniforms for Britain's two great military heroes Lord Nelson and the Duke of Wellington, as well as the uniforms for the Sovereign's personal bodyguard. The company has the distinction of having invented the life-saving waistcoat (an original is on display in their first-floor archive) and famously made the Queen's boat cloak, in which she was photographed in 1953 by Cecil Beaton.

Jigsaw, 159 Mortlake Road, Kew TW9 4AW

The Duchess of Cambridge worked at Jigsaw's head office in Kew as an accessories buyer before her marriage to Prince William. She joined the company, owned by multimillionaires John and Belle Robinson in 2006, working four days a week until she left a year later (she was given an envelope of Jigsaw vouchers). Belle said afterwards: 'Kate supported a couple of Jigsaw events we did. Then she rang me up one day and said, "Could I come and talk to you about work?" She genuinely wanted a job but she needed an element of flexibility to continue the relationship with a very high- profile man and a life that she can't dictate.' Founded by John Robinson in 1969, Jigsaw now has more than 40 stores in the United Kingdom as well as four stores in the States – no two stores are the same. In 2014 it won Drapers 'Retailer of the Year' award.

John Lobb Bootmaker, 9 Saint James' Street, London SW1A 1EF

With two royal warrants from the Duke of Edinburgh and Prince Charles, Lobb's is THE place to get made-to-measure shoes (if you have £2,000 to spare). Both Prince William and Prince Harry are customers of the shop which stands on the spot where Lord Byron had his bachelor pad and was once described by Esquire magazine as 'the most beautiful shop in the world'. Founded in 1863, by John Lobb, a lame Cornish farm boy, who won awards for his cobbling, Lobb's was awarded its first Royal Warrant as Bootmaker to the future Edward VII. Now owned by the fifth generation of Lobbs (one of whom is called William), many of the great and good have had casts made of their feet including Frank Sinatra, Dean Martin, George Bernard Shaw, Roald Dahl, Cole Porter, Lord Oliver, Rex Harrison, Aristole Onassis, Harold Macmillan and Ted Heath.

Patrick Mavros, 104-106 Fulham Road, London SW3 6HS

It is no secret that the Duke and Duchess of Cambridge share a love of Africa: Prince William first visited the country during his gap year and the couple got engaged on a safari holiday in Kenya. So what better gift to mark the birth of their son, than a sterling silver figurine of an African animal? William and Kate's closest friends bought presents for Prince George's christening from jeweller Patrick Mavros, who has shops in London, Harare and Mauritius. The Duchess has long been a fan of Mavros - she discovered him when she was designing jewellery at Jigsaw and bought £70 crocodile stud earrings, £150 Ndoro drop earrings and a £250 Zozo elephant pendant. Kate has since taken her mother and sister to the Fulham Road shop and introduced Prince William and Prince Harry to the designer - she and William are believed to be collecting the firm's miniatures to decorate their apartment in Kensington Palace. The Royals are in good company - author J.K. Rowling bought a silver Mavros dodo and Prince Juan Carlos of Spain asked Mavros to customise the gearstick of his Maybach car with a gold pangolin, which is similar to an anteater. Zimbabwean jeweller Mavros, 60, is not an obvious figure to be attracting such an elevated clientele. But he has gained a cult following among the Royals. He began drawing birds of prey at the age of five in his native Matabeleland, in the western province of Zimbabwe, after he contracted polio and was unable to walk for a year. But it was not until later in life that he began making jewellery. His business has been so successful that his four sons have followed him into the profession: Alexander runs the London store; Forbes, designs jewellery in Mauritius and Pat and Ben are based in Harare.

Peter Jones, Sloane Square, London SW1W 8EL

Home to the Sloane Ranger, Peter Jones is the Duchess of Cambridge's favourite department store – she even popped into the Sloane Street store before her first official evening engagement. Kate is a frequent visitor to the Bobbi Brown make-up counter, where she sat on a stool and had a free lesson on the shop floor (a beautician there is responsible for that 'Scouse brow'). Kate also bought Prince William a pair of £25 Ralph Lauren boxer shorts one Valentine's Day. Peter Jones is owned by the John Lewis Partnership, which opened its first store, a small draper's shop in Oxford Street, in 1864 (it took 16s 4d on the first day). The company also owns Kate's favourite supermarket Waitrose.

Rachel Riley, 82 Marylebone Road, London W1U 4QW

Childrenswear designer Rachel Riley is a favourite of the Duchess of Cambridge and Prince George has been spotted in several of her outfits including the £79 navy sailboat smocked dungarees he wore on his first official engagement in New Zealand and the striped blue polo shirt and matching shorts he wore for his second official outing to Sydney's Taronga Zoo on Easter Sunday. A graduate of Cambridge University and former model, Rachel set up her company, which is inspired by vintage prints, smocking and embroidery, 20 years ago when her children were young. She now has three shops, in Knightsbridge, Marylebone and New York. In 2014 she won 'Best Fashion Retailer' in the Baby & Me Design Awards and 'Best UK Children's Fashion Brand'.

Top: Prince George on his second official royal engagement at Sydney's Taronga Zoo. Above: The sailboat smocked dungarees, which George wore for his first official royal engagement in New Zealand, sold out in an hour. Right: William shares a tender moment with his son.

Richard Ward Salon, 82 Duke of York Square, London SW3 4LY

Celebrity crimper Richard Ward counts the Duchess of Cambridge and Countess of Wessex as clients at his Chelsea salon. But it was his top stylist James Price, who styled Kate's hair for the royal wedding. Renowned for his Chelsea blow dry, Richard also cares for the locks of Carole and Pippa Middleton and the Prime Minister's wife Samantha Cameron. A regular media commentator, he has been awarded the accolade of Fellow with Distinction from the Fellowship for British Hairdressing. He has also designed a detangling Tangle Angel brush.

Shane Connolly, Unit 7, Latimer Road Industrial Estate, Latimer Road, London W10 6RQ

Behind this nondescript door lies the empire of royal warrant holder Shane Connolly, who created the flower arrangements for the royal wedding. In pole position for the job, it was he who designed the displays for Charles' wedding to Camilla Parker-Bowles (he also designed her bouquet). For William and Kate's wedding, Shane, who is known for his eco-friendly floristry, chose eight 20ft high Maple and Hornbeach trees to line the aisle as well as a variety of British flowers such as azaleas, rhododendron, euphorbias, wisteria and lilac. Born and raised in Northern Ireland, Shane read psychology at university before a passion for gardening (which he shares with Prince Charles) led to a change in career. He set up his eponymous company in 1989, and works from a studio in North Kensington.

Smythson, 40 New Bond Street, London W1S 2DE

A favourite of the royal family, the Duchess of Cambridge's Uncle Gary Goldsmith (brother of Carole; godfather of James), popped into Smythson on the day Prince George was born and had his brown leather iPhone case engraved: 'Dad, Husband, Uncle G, Great Uncle G, G.G.' He and daughter Tallulah also bought some Smythson blue writing paper (for a boy) so that the family could write letters to George and put them in a time capsule. The first Smythson store, which opened on Bond Street in 1887, began life supplying calling cards, gilt-edged invitations to coming out balls and tissue-lined envelopes but it made its name with its featherweight diary, which gentlemen carried in their breast pockets. The company soon expanded into supplying travel goods for a generation which enjoyed the golden age of steamboats and motorcars. It still sells stationery – it holds three Royal Warrants – but is perhaps best known for its creative designer, Samantha Cameron, who has made Smythson the place to go to for designer handbags.

The Shop at Bluebird, 350 King's Road, London SW3 5UU

Owned by Jigsaw founders Belle and John Robinson, The Shop at Bluebird was where the Duchess of Cambridge curated her 2007 exhibition Time to Reflect. She and Pippa were guests at the launch of the shop, a boutique below Terence Conran's exclusive eaterie, which once housed Donald Campbell's land speed record-breaking Bluebird car. Kate met portrait photographer Alistair Morrison when she was at St Andrews University and offered to host his exhibition, a series of portraits of stars such as Tom Cruise, Kate Winslet and Ewan McGregor taken in photo booths. Kate's family and friends, including Guy Pelly and Laura Parker Bowles, rallied around and William, who had just arrived back from a secret mission with the Special Boat Service, formed during the Second World War to conduct raids behind German lines in North Africa, with the motto 'By Strength and Guile', made a last-minute appearance. Money raised from the exhibition went to the United Nations children's fund Unicef.

Trotters, 34 King's Road, London SW3 4UD

Prince George's patriotic jumper came from the children's store Trotters, a favourite for Chelsea's Yummy Mummies. The £34.99 navy sweater, which bears a Union Flag, is billed on the company's website as perfect for 'afternoon tea with the Queen'. The company also sells a £19.99 grey cotton T-shirt, emblazoned with guards, and a £14.99 matching soldier hat. Founded by Sophie Mirman and her husband Richard Ross (who set up Tie Rack and the Sock Shop), Trotters was the first children's store when it opened its doors in 1990. The family-owned business now has six shops, as well as a hairdressing salon for children. Sophie, whose mother was a royal milliner, has won many awards including Business Woman of the Year, Marketing Woman of the Year and Motivator of the Year.

Turnbull & Asser, 71-2 Jermyn Street, London SW1Y 6PF

When Prince Charles broke his arm playing polo, he turned to Turnbull & Asser to create his tailored sling – the prince is a fan of their shirts (he visited their Gloucester factory in 2013 as part of a 'Best of English' tour and even tried sewing a shirt). Prince William and Prince Harry have worn Turnbull & Asser creations since they were children. They are in good company – the Beatles bought their pyjamas at Turnbull & Asser and Frank Sinatra ordered bespoke shirts, which buttoned under the crotch with a Quorn strap (originally designed for hunting). The company, which has been in existence since 1885, was awarded its first Royal Warrant by Edward VII.

SPORT

All England Lawn Tennis and Croquet Club, Church Road, London SW19 5AE

A keen tennis fan, the Duchess of Cambridge has been a regular in the Royal Box at Wimbledon since she got married. She and William joined in a Mexican wave and led the royal box in a standing ovation in 2011 after Andy Murray roared into the quarter-final in straight sets (he lost in the semi-final to Nadal). The following year the couple braved the rain to watch Murray make it to the semi-final (he lost to Federer in the finals). Kate exchanged kisses with Tim Henman's mother Jane, William shook hands with her husband Tony, and Tim, who was commentating for the BBC, joked: 'They let anyone in the Royal Box these days.' The couple stayed away from Wimbledon in 2013 and missed Andy Murray's historic win against Djokovic, becoming the first British man to win the Championships since Fred Perry in 1936 (he also won the Olympic gold the previous year). But they were back in 2014 (with Carole and Michael Middleton) to watch the defending champion crash out of Wimbledon in the quarter final to Grigor Dimitrov. One of four Grand Slam tennis tournaments, the Wimbledon Championships is the oldest tennis tournament in the world. It has been held at the All England Club since 1877.

Below: Kate and William enjoy a day at the All England Lawn Tennis Club.

GSK Human Performance Lab, Brentford TW8 9DA

Two years after Britain's Olympic success at London 2012, the Duchess of Cambridge, who is patron of SportsAid, met the next generation of sporting hopefuls and their coaches, during a workshop at one of the world's top sports laboratories, the GlaxoSmithKline Human Performance Laboratory (HPL). The group was assessed on respiration, temperature, power, cognition and body composition but Kate, who was 16 weeks pregnant, was restricted to testing her brain rather than her body. After being given two cognitive exercises, to measure her reactions, she joked: 'Finally something I can do while I am pregnant.' The GSKHPL is a world-class science facility which seeks to deepen their understanding of sporting prowess by testing six pillars of human performance: strength, stamina, cognition, hydration, metabolism and recovery.

Queen Elizabeth Olympic Park, London E20 2ST

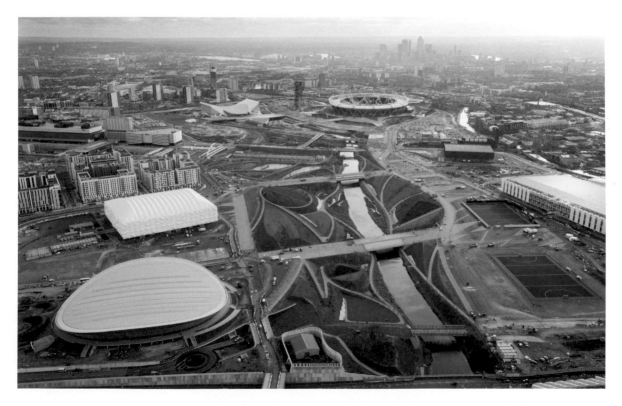

Top: GSK. Above: The Queen Elizabeth Olympic Park.

The Duke and Duchess of Cambridge and Prince Harry were regular faces at the Queen Elizabeth Olympic Park during the 2012 London Olympics. The trio attended more than 30 events as Official Ambassadors for Team GB during that summer. William and Kate attended the opening ceremony at the Olympic Stadium - in which the Queen made her film debut in a James Bond stunt - while Kate and Harry attended the closing ceremony (William was on duty as an RAF Search and Rescue pilot). The Duke and Duchess also watched Rebecca Adlington defend her 800-metre swimming title at the London Aquatics Centre, gasped with disbelief when Victoria Pendleton and her partner Jess Varnish were disqualified from the women's sprint at the Velodrome and embraced when Sir Chris Hoy landed his fifth gold medal in the men's team sprint. Kate, who was captain of the hockey team at Marlborough, also watched the British women's hockey team win their first Olympic medal in 20 years at the Riverbank Arena. Since the London Olympics, the 56-acre Queen Elizabeth Olympic Park, which is the same size as Hyde Park, has been transformed at a cost of £300 million. William and Harry attended the launch of the Invictus Games there – with Prince Charles and the Duchess of Cornwall – in 2014. The stadium will be the new home of West Ham United Football Club.

Below: William and Kate celebrate Sir Chris Hoy and Team GB winning Olympic Gold.

Twickenham Stadium, Whitton Road, Twickenham TW2 7BA

The Duke and Duchess of Cambridge were among the spectators at Twickenham in 2007 when England beat Italy in the Six Nations Championship. The couple was joined by Prince Harry at the home of England Rugby. Twickenham, which now seats 82,000 people began life as a humble cabbage patch. The RFU bought the land for £5,500 in 1907 and the first game – a battle between Harlequins and Richmond – was played in 1909. The stadium is now the largest dedicated ruby union venue in the world – it also doubles as a music venue (U2, Bon Jovi and the Rolling Stones have all performed there), offers stadium tours and is home to the World Rugby Museum.

Wembley Stadium, Wembley HA9 0WS

As President of The Football Association, Prince William has been a regular visitor to Wembley Stadium (in 2014 he chatted to then captain Steven Gerrard and players Wayne Rooney and Daniel Sturridge in the dressing room after they beat Peru 3-0 in an England friendly). But his most memorable appearance was at the Concert for Diana that he and Harry organised on what would have been their mother's 46th birthday – ten years after her death. The 2007 concert was memorable because it was the moment that he and Kate were reunited publicly for the first time since they had split 12 weeks earlier. Sir Elton John, who wrote the Princess Diana tribute song 'Candle in the Wind 1997', opened the gig with a rendition of his classic 'Your Song' before introducing the two princes to the audience. To a standing ovation, William and Harry took to the stage. 'Hello, Wembley!' shouted Harry. 'This evening is about all that our mother loved in life: her music, her dancing, her charities, and her family and friends,' added William, before introducing Duran Duran, one of Diana's favourite bands, telling the crowd to 'have an awesome time'. William and Kate sat two rows apart in the royal box during the concert (they did not look at each other once) but afterwards, at the £250,000 back-stage party, William made a beeline for Kate and they spent the rest of the evening together, kissing passionately on the dance floor and dancing to their favourite song the BodyRockers' hit I Like the Way You Move. The new 90,000 seat Wembley Stadium, which was built by the Australian firm Multiplex at a cost of £798 million, opened in 2007. It is the second largest stadium in Europe and the largest in the United Kingdom.

Westway Sports Centre, 1 Crowthorne Road, London W10 6RP

The Duke of Cambridge joined a volleyball game in 2013 when he visited Westway Sports Centre with Prince Harry – but he failed to return any balls. The royal princes were watching an apprentice training session, organised by Coach Core, an initiative they set up to encourage youngsters from disadvantaged backgrounds to become sports coaches. Afterwards William told that them he expected to see them in the Premiership or the Olympics 'coaching the next gold medal winners'. Coach Core has two pilot projects, one in London, run by the charity Greenhouse, and one in Glasgow, run by Glasgow Life.

Top: Twickenham Stadium. Above left and middle: William chats to Wayne Rooney, Daniel Sturridge and Steven Gerrard. Left: William plays volleyball at Westway Sports Centre.

TRANSPORT

Baker Street tube station, Marylebone Road, London NW1 5LA

She was unlikely to use it – but the Duchess of Cambridge was still given a 'Baby on Board badge' when she went on a tour of Baker Street tube station with the Queen and the Duke of Edinburgh. Kate, who was five months pregnant, turned to the Monarch and joked: 'I will have to wear it at home.' The Queen did not leave empty handed either: she was presented with a commemorative Oyster card. The royal party was visiting Baker Street to mark the 150th anniversary of London Underground (the station was on the first stretch of the network, which opened in 1863 between Paddington and Farringdon). After meeting workers in the ticket hall, the royals moved downstairs to Platform 1 on the North bound Metropolitan Line, where they looked around a new S7 train, which has walk through carriages and air conditioning. The sovereign later unveiled a plaque, naming the train 'Queen Elizabeth II', and, to the delight of Prince Philip, the group was invited to view a restored 1892 'Jubilee' coach, the oldest operational carriage in the world. It was the first time the Queen had been on London Underground since May 1939 when she travelled on a tube with her sister Princess Margaret and their governess. Kate was a regular tube traveller until her marriage.

Routemaster Bus, London

The Duke and Duchess of Cambridge surprised commuters in Kensington High Street in the run up to Remembrance Sunday by hopping off a Routemaster bus. The couple greeted volunteers on the bus, who were selling poppies in aid of the Royal British Legion London Poppy Day, in 2013, in a bid to raise £1 million in 24 hours. The iconic Routemaster bus, which had a conductor, was first seen on the streets of London in 1954 but it was retired from general service for safety reasons in 2005. However a new Routemaster bus – inspired by the original - is back in the capital. The first prototypes were tried on route 38 in February 2012.

Above: a pregnant Kate visits Baker Street tube station. Right: a London Routemaster bus on Westminster Bridge.

EAST OF ENGLAND

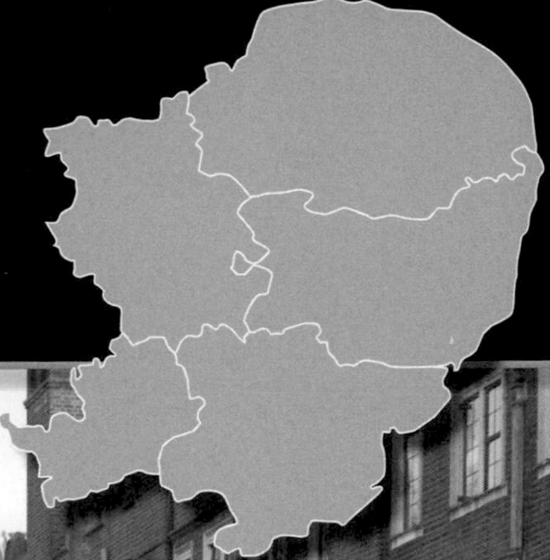

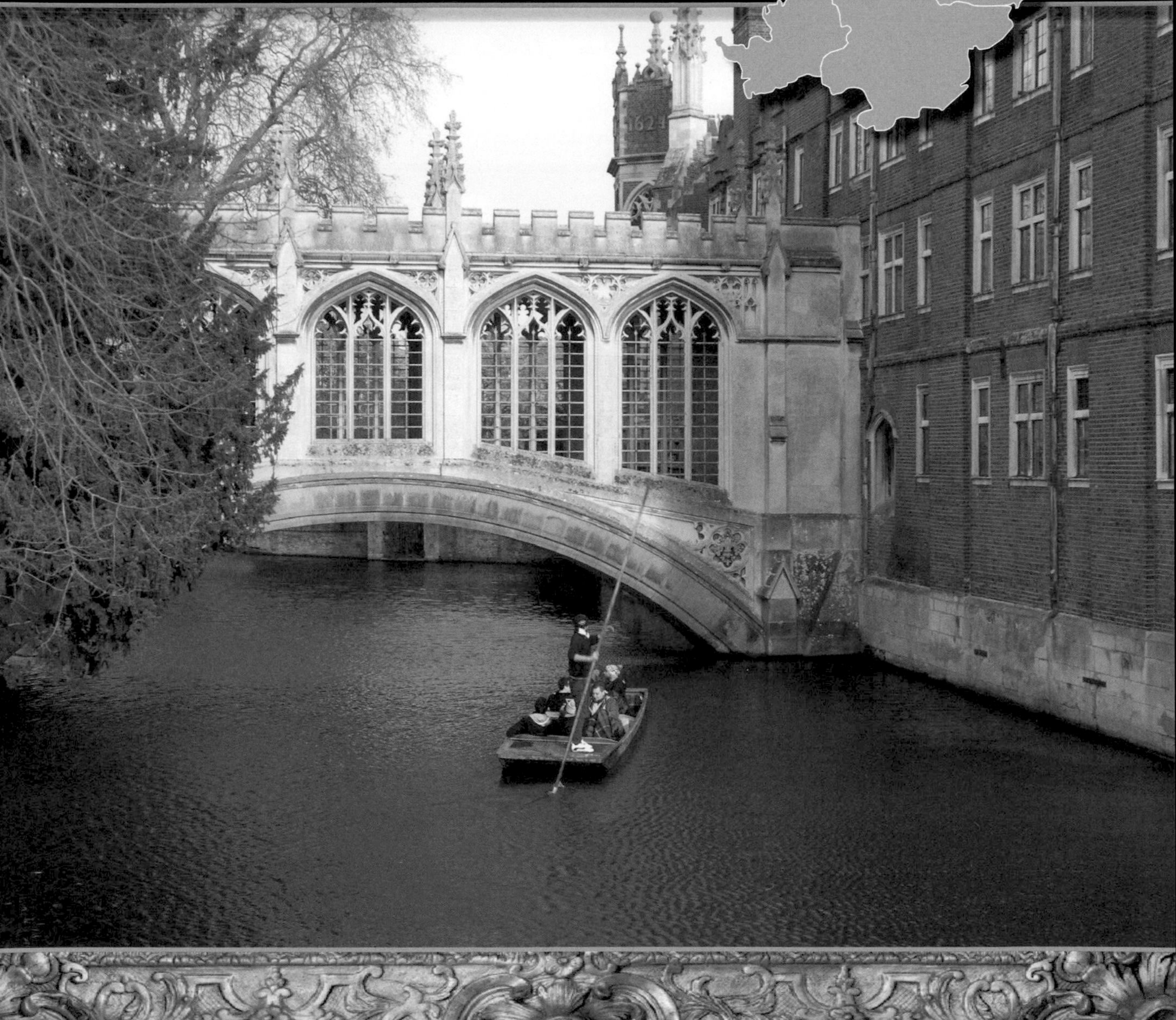

CAMBRIDGESHIRE

CAMBRIDGE

Cambridge International Airport, Newmarket Road, Cambridge CB5 8RX

The Guildhall, Market Square, Cambridge CB2 3QJ

Jimmy's Cambridge, 1 East Road, Cambridge CB1 1BD

North Cambridge Academy, Abury Road, Cambridge CB4 2JF

Senate House, King's Parade, Cambridge CB2 1ST

St John's College, St Johns St, Cambridge CB2 1TP

Trinity College, Cambridge CB2 1TQ

Previous page: St John's College, Cambridge. Above: William signs the register at The Guildhall watched by Mayor of Cambridge Cllr Shelia Stuart.

Both the Duke and Duchess of Cambridge have historic links to Cambridge – as well as their titles – so it was unsurprising that they made a whistle stop tour of the city, which bears their name, the year after they got married. It was in Cambridge that William sparked rumours that Kate was pregnant after accepting a baby grow, bearing a picture of a helicopter under the slogan 'Daddy's little co-pilot'. William and Kate toured Cambridge in 2012, starting at The Guildhall (or town hall), which was designed by architect Charles Cowles-Voysey in 1939, where they met the Mayor of Cambridge, Cllr Sheila Stuart, and the High Sheriff, and appeared on a balcony, overlooking the market square, to wave at the 4,000-strong crowd. On leaving the building, they did a walkabout on their way to Cambridge University's 18th century Senate House, which is now used for degree ceremonies, where they met some of the students.

The couple then opened Jimmy's new £3 million homeless shelter, named after Jim Dilley, who spent much of his life sleeping rough, ending his years under a bridge over the M11 motorway – he died in Papworth Hospital in 1994 from lung cancer and his ashes were scattered at Junction 13. Originally based in the basement of Zion Baptist Church, the centre now operates from a four-storey building. Finally they visited Manor Community College – now North Cambridge Academy – where William gave pupil Hollie Dean a hug, making her the 'luckiest girl in Cambridge'. Kate's great-great grandfather Francis Lupton went up to Trinity College, Cambridge, in the 19th century (it became a traditional rite of passage for Lupton sons) while Prince Charles followed his grandfather, George VI, to Trinity in 1967. Even William, who famously met Kate at St Andrews University, did a ten-week 'bespoke' course in agriculture at Cambridge University in 2014. Run by the Cambridge Programme for Sustainability Leadership and based in the Department of Land Economy (dubbed by students the 'Department of Grass Management', he took some of his tutorials at St John's College. Both colleges have an illustrious history dating from the 15th century. St John's is the earlier of the two, founded in 1511, by Lady Margaret Beaufort, the mother of Henry VII, who wanted to transform the ancient hospital of St John the Evangelist, into a college for students in the liberal arts and technology – she died in 1509 so the foundation charter was sealed by her executors (alumni include the social reformer William Wilberforce, the poet William Wordsworth and the athlete Christopher Brasher). Trinity College's history dates from the reign of Henry VIII, who founded the college in 1546, combining Michaelhouse and King's Hall. Its library, created by Sir Christopher Wren, contains many treasures, the oldest of which is an 8th century copy of the Epistles of St Paul, and its students rank among the greatest – 32 Nobel Prizewinners and six Prime Ministers have graduated from the college.

Above: William and Kate meet Pete at Jimmy's £3m homeless shelter.

Cambridge will see much more of William and Kate now that they have moved to their country home, Anmer Hall. William has taken up a two-year job as an East Anglian Air Ambulance pilot, based at Cambridge International Airport. On a salary of £40,000 a year, he is the first direct heir to the throne to be an ordinary employee on PAYE (he is donating his salary to charity).

Milton

East Anglia's Children's Hospice, Church Lane, Milton, Cambridgeshire CB24 6AB

The Duchess of Cambridge recorded her first video message during Children's Hospice Week after being inspired by her visit to East Anglia's Children's Hospice (EACH). Kate made a private visit to EACH, in 2011, and chose the charity, which has three hospices in Milton, Ipswich and Quidenham, as one of her patronages. She later said: 'When I first visited the hospice in Milton, far from being a clinical, depressing place for sick children, it was a home. Most importantly, it was a family home, a happy place of stability, support and care. It was a place of fun.'

Above: St John's College, Cambridge, founded in 1511.

ESSEX

CHELMSFORD

Hylands Park, London Road, Chelmsford, Essex CM2 8WQ

The biggest event in the history of Scouting was held at Hylands Park in 2007 – and Prince William (who has never been a Scout himself) was in the 40,000-strong crowd. He joined the Duke of Kent, who is patron of The Scout Association, at the 21st World Scout Jamboree, which was held on the centenary of the movement, which was founded by Lord Baden-Powell. The scouts, from more than 160 countries, were housed in a 'tent town' but William arrived by helicopter, to the cheers of the crowd. He was presented with a traditional neckerchief, commemorating the jamboree, which he hung around his neck. Founded in 1907 - the first camp was set up on Brownsea Island in Dorset   the Scouting Movement now has 28 million members. The Duchess of Cambridge has now taken over William's mantle and is a high-profile volunteer. Hylands House is a stunning Grade II* listed property, which has been restored to its former glory and is situated in 574 acres of historic landscaped parkland.

Above: the Grade II* listed Hylands House, set in 574 acres of landscaped parkland.

HERTFORDSHIRE

LEAVESDEN

Warner Bros Studios, Warner Drive, Leavesden, Hertfordshire WD25 7LP

Leavesden is now the home of Warner Bros Studios, the first film studio to be built in the UK for 70 years, and the only Hollywood studio in Britain. The Duke and Duchess of Cambridge, who was six months pregnant, and Prince Harry visited the new £100 million building in

2013 for its inauguration and were given a tour of the Harry Potter set, which was created at the old Leavesden Studios. After each being given a wand – and taught a few spell techniques – they were invited to duel (Kate successfully took on her husband). The trio, who were accompanied by 500 guests and children associated with their charities, were then shown props from the Batman film The Dark Knight Rises including the Batmobile and Bat Bike. 'We should borrow that for the weekend,' William whispered to Harry, before climbing inside the car and revving the engine. To the obvious jealousy of his brother, he then jumped on board the Bat Bike. Originally built in 1939, as a warehouse for the Ministry of Defence to make aircraft such as the Mosquito fighter and Halifax bomber, the site was bought by Rolls Royce after WWII and converted into an aircraft engine factory. When they closed in 1992, it became Leavesden Film Studios, where all eight Harry Potter films were made, as well as the James Bond movie Goldeneye and Star Wars Episode One: The Phantom Menace. Warner Bros new state-of-the-art studios now encompass nine sound stages, a 100-acre back-lot and one of the largest underwater filming tanks in Europe.

Left: the Harry Potter set at Warner Bros Studios.

NORFOLK

ANMER

Anmer Hall, Anmer, Norfolk PE31 6RW

Above: William and Kate's Norfolk home, Anmer Hall, which was a gift from the Queen.

Nestled in the heart of the Norfolk countryside, down a long sweeping driveway, lined with trees and shrubs to shield it from prying eyes, lies one of the most famous Georgian manor houses in Britain. Built at the turn of the 19th century in red brick, with a semi-circular porch on two Tuscan columns and a clay pantile roof (currently bright orange until it weathers), Anmer Hall is the new family home of the Duke and Duchess of Cambridge.

The couple were gifted the ten-bedroom mansion, which has a swimming pool and tennis courts, by the Queen. One of 150 properties on the monarch's 20,000-acre Sandringham Estate, it lies only two miles east of Sandringham House - one of her favourite private residences, where the royals celebrate Christmas every year. It is a house steeped in royal history: not only was it the home to one of Camilla Parker Bowles' ancestors but it was the location of her illicit trysts with Prince Charles - that's not to mention the Queen's cousin, the Duke of Kent, and Prince Charles' university pal, Hugh van Cutsem. Although it has illustrious pedigree, it was originally a private residence. The future Edward VII only bought the property in 1896 – five years before he ascended the throne – and Anmer Hall became a grace-and-favour home.

Its first tenant was the bushy-bearded Admiral Sir Frederick Tower Hamilton, a former Aide-de-Camp to Edward VII, who had fought in the Zulu War. His wife Maria was the daughter of Sir Henry Keppel, the younger brother of the Duchess of Cornwall's great-great-great grandfather George Keppel, 6th Earl of Albermarle, who was Camilla's first cousin four times removed. Other renowned residents of Anmer Hall include Sir John Maffey, the grandfather of Britain's disgraced former Conservative cabinet minister Jonathan Aitken and actress Maria Aitken, the Queen's cousin the Duke of Kent – who lived there with his wife and three children (The Earl of St Andrews, Lady Helen Taylor and Lord Nicholas Windsor) and Prince Charles' university friend Hugh van Cutsem (father of Edward, Hugh, Nicholas and William). It is reputedly the country bolthole where Charles enjoyed secret trysts with his then mistress Camilla Parker Bowles. William and Kate have spent an estimated £1.5 million putting their stamp on the property and shielding it from intruders and paparazzi: they have built a new driveway across a grazing field, installed a gate across a public road and re-routed the approach road to the nearby St Mary's Church for worshippers. They have also built a new glass-roofed garden room, linking the main house to an old wood store, which has been transformed into a 'nanny flat', converted a garage block into accommodation for royal protection officers and installed a top-of-the-range kitchen. Tourists can take a guided tour around Sandringham but nobody without an embossed invitation will dine at Anmer Hall.

CASTLE RISING

Castle Rising Castle, Castle Rising, King's Lynn, Norfolk PE31 6AH

The village of Castle Rising, which is the home of one of the most famous 12th century castles in England, became the venue for a 'friendly' when Princes William and Harry joined estate workers from Sandringham for a football match on Boxing Day 2013. Despite the friendly banter, the two brothers, who were on opposing teams, were obviously keen to win as they bashed into each other several times on the rain-sodden pitch. But at the end of the second half the score was 2-2 and the princes proved they were good sports by hugging after the final whistle. Built in 1138 by the Norman baron William d'Aubigny for his new wife Adeliza – the widowed second wife of Henry I – Castle Rising Castle has served as a hunting lodge and a royal residence. It was the exile of Queen Isabella, widow – and alleged murderess of Edward II – and mother of Edward III before passing into the hands of the Howard family in the 16th century.

Left: William and Harry hug after playing a game of football on opposing teams at Castle Rising.

EAST RAYNHAM

St Mary's Church, Raynham Park, East Raynham, Norfolk NR21 7ER

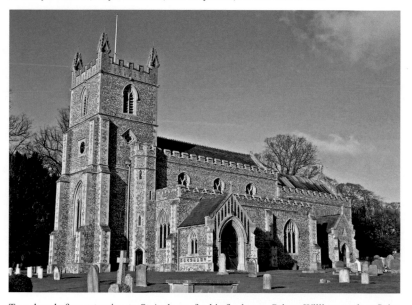

Two days before returning to St Andrews for his final year, Prince William made a flying visit to East Raynham to attend the wedding of his distant cousin Davina Duckworth Chad and old Etonian Tom Barber. He arrived in a minibus with Prince Harry and was joined by their uncle Earl Spencer, a cousin of Davina's mother Elizabeth, who had chosen the boys' mother Princess Diana to be her own bridesmaid 35 years earlier. Davina, who once posed for Country Life magazine's website in a revealing rubber dress, earning herself the nickname 'the Deb on the Web', was invited on the ten-day Mediterranean 'love boat' cruise with the royals in 1999. A history of art graduate, she kept in touch with the princes after she left Bristol University and went to work at the West End art gallery owned by Lady Helen Taylor's husband Tim. St Mary's Church, which was rebuilt in 1868 (it retains the 15th century Easter Sepulchre) stands in the park of Raynham Hall.

FAKENHAM

Thursford Collection, Thursford, Fakenham, Norfolk NR21 0AS

Above right: the 19th century St Mary's Church. Above: Prince George met Santa at the Thursford Collection.

With its Christmas Spectacular and Santa's Magical Journey, the Thursford Collection, 20 miles from Sandringham, has hosted Prince William twice. In 2010 he attended a Christmas Spectacular and Reception in aid of the Teenager Cancer Trust and four years later, he and the Duchess of Cambridge took Prince George to tour its Winter Wonderland. George clapped his hands in excitement as he saw animated reindeer, penguins, polar bears and elves in the fake snow and sparkling lights. But the highlight of his visit was toddling into see Father Christmas, who gave him a wooden train.

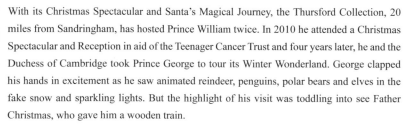

GAYTON

Gayton Hall, Gayton, Norfolk PE32 1PL
St Nicholas' Church, Lynn Road, Gayton, Norfolk PE32 1PA

With its stunning 20-acre water garden – the grounds include woodland, lakes, streams and bridges - the Georgian mansion house Gayton Hall was the ideal venue for the 2013 wedding reception of William's friends James Meade and Lady Laura Marsham. Owned by her father Julian Marsham, 8th Earl of Romney, the hall (its gardens are open to the public) is directly opposite St Nicholas' Church, with its domed tower, where the couple married and guests – including ushers Princes William and Harry and Pippa Middleton walked straight across a field to the party. Meade, known as 'Badger', the old Etonian son of Olympic gold medal event rider, Richard, delivered a joint speech with Thomas van Straubenzee at the royal wedding. His wife is involved with the Tusk Trust, a conservation charity of which William is patron. St Nicholas' Church can be seen from all roads approaching the village. On its four corners are the much-weathered emblems of the evangelists – the winged man for St Matthew; a lion for St Mark; an ox for St Luke and an eagle for St John.

Above left: William strolls across a field to the wedding reception.
Left: St Nicholas' Church. Top: the Georgian mansion Gayton Hall.

GREAT MASSINGHAM

The Dabbling Duck, 11 Abbey Road, Great Massingham, Norfolk PE32 2HN

The Dabbling Duck's battle to remain open – and not be converted into housing – was rewarded when Prince William popped into the pub in 2013. William was one of 15 ushers who travelled five miles to the pub in a shooting party trailer for a pre-wedding breakfast – or pub lunch – before the nuptials of Lady Laura Marsham and James Meade. The pub, which is situated between two large ponds, is named after its 'dabbling ducks' from the children's book The Wind In the Willows ('ducks go a dabbling – up tails all')

HOLT

Mews Antique Emporium, 5-6 Manor Mews, Holt, Norfolk NR25 6AW

When the Duchess of Cambridge was renovating her country home, Anmer Hall, she enjoyed browsing in the antique shops in the nearby market town of Holt. She popped into Mews Antique Emporium in 2013 with some friends and reportedly bought a sideboard and a three-legged table.

NORWICH

Norfolk Showground, Dereham Road, Costessey, Norwich, Norfolk NR5 0TT

Top and above right: the Dabbling Duck. Above: Kate is given a posy at Norfolk showground.

The Duchess of Cambridge threw protocol to the wind when she visited Norwich Showground in 2014 for the East Anglia's Children's Hospices £10 million Nook Appeal. Moved to tears after listening to physiotherapist Leigh Smith talking about the death of her three-month-old daughter Beatrice, she spontaneously gave her a hug. Kate, who was 18 weeks pregnant with her second child, had already given some comfort to Leigh, who had written to her after the death of the three-month-old by sending a hand-written reply. Kate, who is patron of the charity, also unveiled a range of Emma Bridgewater mugs, which are being sold for the appeal – she approached the potter personally on the charity's behalf. Set in glorious parkland, Norfolk Showground, which is owned by the Royal Norfolk Agricultural Association, is home to the world renowned Royal Norfolk Show - the largest two-day agricultural show in the United Kingdom.

SANDRINGHAM

The Sandringham Estate, Sandringham, Norfolk PE35 6EN

Above and opposite: the Sandringham Estate in Norfolk where the Royals spend Christmas. Breaking with tradition, William and Kate spend alternative years with the Royals and the Middletons.

The Duchess of Cambridge's first visit to the Queen's Norfolk country home was for a shooting party in 2002, hosted by Prince William at Wood Farm, a modest cottage, set in a secluded corner of the Sandringham Estate. She was one of six girls and ten boys – including the prince – crammed into the six-bedroom cottage, which was once home to Prince John, the youngest son of George V. Since then she has visited the estate regularly – although she has only stayed in Sandringham House, the Queen's private residence, since she married William. Traditionally the royal family gather in Norfolk for the festive season - William and Kate spent their first Christmas as man and wife with the royal family in 2011 (the Duke of Edinburgh missed the celebrations because he was having an operation on a blocked artery) but in a break with tradition, they have been spending alternate years with the royals. In 2012, they spent the holiday with the Middleton family as Kate was suffering from hyperemesis gravidarum, an extreme form of morning sickness, and in 2014 the couple invited the Middletons to stay with them at Anmer Hall, attending church with the royal family before heading back to their own home for lunch. Sandringham House, set in 59 acres of stunning grounds, at the heart of the 20,000-acre estate, has been the private home of four generations of royals since the future Edward VII bought the house and furnishings for £220,000 in 1862, the year before he married Princess Alexandra of Denmark. He devised the idea of Sandringham Time (ST) to make the most of the winter daylight hours and his passion for shooting so the clocks all over the estate were advanced by half an hour (George V maintained the tradition but it was abolished by Edward VIII). George V also lived at Sandringham, moving into a house on the estate, which came to be known as York Cottage, after he married Princess Mary of Teck. He referred to Sandringham as 'the place I love better than anywhere in the world.' The couple remained in the cottage after he succeeded to the throne, moving to the 'Big House' in 1925 after his mother died. There he presided over a new Christmas Day tradition – the first Christmas broadcast to the Empire went live in 1932 (the Queen made history again in 1957 when she broadcast the first televised broadcast). Edward VIII spent only one day at Sandringham in his brief reign – he sold the estate to his brother after his abdication. The new George VI loved the estate as much as his father, spending many months a year there. He died in his sleep in Sandringham House in 1952. It is now a family tradition that the royals spend Christmas at Sandringham, attending a private family service at St Mary Magdalene Church – in 2014 the Duke and Duchess of Cambridge arrived hand in hand for the traditional service but they left Prince George at home. The 16th century parish church is a country church with an exceptional history – there are memorials to many members of the royal family. American Rodman Wanamaker presented Queen Alexandra with a silver altar, silver pulpit and silver 17th century Spanish processional cross as a tribute to King Edward VII. The church has a sumptuous chancel, decorated with carved angels, a Florentine marble font, Greek 9th century font and 16th century stained glass.

SNETTISHAM

St Mary's Church, Old Church Road, Snettisham, Norfolk PE31 7LX

It is not normal to be invited to a stranger's wedding – let alone royal nuptials – but that is what happened to holiday makers Josie Williams and Wendy Ablett when they were exploring St Mary's Church. They stumbled across the 2009 wedding of Prince William's cousin Laura Fellowes to city banker Nick Pettman – which was attended by Prince William, the Duchess of Cambridge, and Earl Spencer - and were given last-minute invitations. The 14th century church, which was described by historian Nikolaus Pevsner as 'perhaps the most exciting decorated church in Norfolk', has the unusual accolade of being the model for two Canadian cathedrals – in Fredericton and Montreal. It is also the first church in the country to have been hit by a German bomb – it was dropped in a nearby field in 1915 and most of the south and east windows were shattered. Its 175-spire is a local landmark.

TATTERSETT

Pynkney Hall, Tattersett, Norfolk PE31 6TF

The Grade II listed Pynkney Hall is the home of landowner Anthony Duckworth-Chad, who is a close friend of the Prince of Wales, and was the venue for his only daughter Davina's wedding reception to Tom Barber after the ceremony at St Mary's Church, in East Raynham. Prince William and Prince Harry were among the 300 guests at the former debutante's reception, which was held two days before William's final year at St Andrews, but Kate did not attend. Pynkney Hall was originally founded in 1587 but its current building, a country house with a mid-Georgian north front and Queen Anne style south front, dates from the 17th century. Remnants of a medieval moat still survive.

Above : the 14th century St Mary's Church, described by historian Nikolaus Pevsner as 'perhaps the most exciting decorated church in Norfolk'.
Right: originally founded in 1587, Pynkney Hall still boasts remnants of a medieval moat.

SUFFOLK

FRESSINGFIELD

Fox and Goose, Church Road, Fressingfield, Suffolk IP21 5PB

The owner of the Fox and Goose pub has the distinction of cooking for the future King and Queen. Paul Yaxley, who has been awarded two AA Rosettes and features in the Michelin guide, did the catering for the 2012 wedding of Kate's old school friend Hannah Gillingham in the nearby village of Wingfield. 'We didn't find out until the day that William and Kate were going to be there' he said afterwards. 'It's a huge honour to be able to say I have cooked for the future King.'

Above and right: the Fox and Goose in Fressingfield.

IPSWICH

The Treehouse Centre, St Augustine's Gardens, Ipswich, Suffolk IP3 8NS

One of three hospices run by East Anglia's Children's Hospices, the Treehouse was formally opened by its patron the Duchess of Cambridge in 2012 after a £3 million fundraising appeal. Kate toured the hospice, planted a tree, was given a posy by six-year-old Tilly Jennings, who had a rare heart condition, and made her first public speech. 'The Treehouse is all about family and fun,' she said. 'For many, this is a home from home — a lifeline, enabling families to live as normally as possible, during a very precious period of time. What you do is inspirational, it's a shining example of the support and care that is delivered, not just here, but in the children's hospice movement at large, up and down the country. The feelings you inspire — feelings of love and of hope — offer a chance to families to live a life they never thought could be possible.'

Top: Kate shows her artistic streak to children at The Treehouse. Left: Kate makes her first public speech.

WESTLETON

The Westleton Crown, The Street, Westleton, Nr Southwold, Suffolk IP17 3AD

Top and above: William and Kate spent the night before their first wedding anniversary at The Crown Inn.

This 12th century coaching inn was where the Duke and Duchess of Cambridge spent the night before their first wedding anniversary. The couple was among a group of friends staying at the pub after the 2012 wedding of Hannah Gillingham and Robert Carter. They arrived and had a glass of champagne with the other guests, who included Pippa Middleton, before retiring to the £165-a-night Swan Room, which had a four-poster bed and a 'stylish roll top bath big enough for two'. On their anniversary they dined on a full English breakfast in the pub's garden restaurant before leaving late morning and returning to Anglesey where Kate reportedly cooked William fish en papillote (she chose the parchment – or paper – to symbolise their first year together). Manager Gareth Clarke said afterwards: 'They're the first royalty we've had staying with us. It's not every day you welcome the second in line to the throne. It was certainly a surprise to all the team when they arrived. We were made aware that some special guests were arriving but we didn't know just how special.'

WINGFIELD

De La Pole Arms, Church Road, Wingfield, Norfolk IP21 5RA
St Andrew's Church, Church Road, Wingfield, Suffolk IP21 5RA

The Duke and Duchess of Cambridge made five-year-old Grace Radbourne's week when they popped into the De La Pole Arms with their dog Lupo, before they went to Hannah Gillingham's 2012 wedding on the day before their first wedding anniversary. While Kate chatted to Grace, William joked to her parents Helen and Nick that it was a 'nice day for it' - even though it was pouring with rain. Afterwards Helen said: 'They were very relaxed and friendly. Kate went up to Grace and had a little chat and William said 'hello' to my husband and made a joke about it being 'a nice day for it' because it was pouring down. Grace thought it was amazing. She's been a very popular girl at school this week after her brush with royalty.' Later the couple joined other guests at the church, which was built in the 14th century by Sir John de Wingfield, who was chief of staff to the Black Prince, the eldest son of Edward III. (in 2012 it celebrated the 650th anniversary of its foundation). Kate, and sister Pippa, have known Hannah since they were all pupils at Marlborough College – they played hockey, netball and tennis together.

Top: the 14th century St Andrew's Church.
Above: William and Kate popped into the
De La Pole Arms with their dog Lupo.

EAST MIDLANDS

DERBYSHIRE

BAKEWELL

Chatsworth House, Bakewell, Derbyshire DE45 1PP

William's first job as a working royal began in October 2005, when he arrived at Chatsworth, seat of the Duke and Duchess of Devonshire and one of Britain's grandest stately homes. He spent the next two weeks in the Peak District learning how to manage the 35,000-acre estate, even working behind the scenes in its award-winning butcher's shop. Wearing a traditional apron and straw boater, he joined the other backroom workers weighing the heavy cuts of meat. But he and his two police detectives lived in more luxurious surroundings than his fellow workers, staying in a 16th century hunting tower overlooking Capability Brown's stunning park. Originally built as a summer banqueting house from which ladies could watch their gentlemen hunting, the 400ft turret with its narrow spiral staircase had been restored earlier that year to accommodate paying guests, although William was let off the £900-a-week rent. It was a plum first job for the prince, who has inherited his father's love of the environment and has always harboured a desire to be a gentleman farmer. In the visitors' book, which he signed 'Will, Gloucestershire', he wrote: 'A wonderful place to stay but don't try to tackle the stairs once you have a drink!' Chatsworth House dates back to the Elizabethan era when Elizabeth Talbot, Countess of Shrewsbury, known as Bess of Hardwick, persuaded her second husband Sir William Cavendish (she was married four times) to move to her home country. They bought Chatsworth manor in 1549 for £600 and began to build a house – the hunting tower, where William stayed, still stands to this day. William Cavendish, 1st Earl of Devonshire, who was Bess' favourite son, inherited the house in 1608 on his mother's death. The estate is now run by the Chatsworth House Trust, a charitable foundation which was established by Andrew Cavendish, 11th Duke, who lived at Chatsworth, with his wife, the Hon Deborah Mitford, and their three children.

Previous page and top: Chatsworth House, which dates back to the Elizabethan era. Above: its grand staircase.

LEICESTERSHIRE

FLECKNEY

Fiona Cairns, 36 Churchill Way, Fleckney, Leicestershire LE8 8UD

When graphic designer and pastry chef Fiona Cairns made a batch of miniature fruit cakes (in baked bean cans) for friends one Christmas, she could never have imagined that a quarter of a century later she would create the Duke and Duchess of Cambridge's wedding cake. The eight-tiered cake, made by a team of chefs in two months, from 17 fruitcakes, was baked and decorated with 900 sugar-paste flowers in this Leicestershire bakery, and was displayed in the Summer Exhibition at Buckingham Palace. William and Kate have reputedly saved the top three layers for themselves – suggesting three christenings. Fiona, who has now written three books and hosted ITV's The Home of Fabulous Cakes, studied graphic design at university before beginning her career in illustration. It was only after she got married to husband Kishore that she did a cookery course at La Petit Cuisine, in Richmond, south west London. She went on to work as a pastry chef at the Michelin-starred restaurant at Hambleton Hall, in Rutland. After making some cakes for Christmas presents, she began marketing her designs and got her first order for 72 miniature cakes from the Conran Shop. As the business grew (she now supplies Harrods, Selfridges, Fortnum & Mason and Paris' Le Bon Marche), the couple converted a barn in their garden into a bakery before moving out into a state-of-the-art bakery in Fleckney.

LEICESTER

De Montfort University, The Gateway, Leicester LE1 9BH

As Prince William was in the Falklands, the Queen and the Duke of Edinburgh invited the Duchess of Cambridge to launch her 2012 Diamond Jubilee Tour. It was the first time that Kate had taken part in an official engagement without her husband. The trio travelled on a scheduled train from St Pancras to Leicester, where they visited the city's De Montfort University, where the Queen and the Duchess watched a fashion show. Kate was invited to choose one the winner of six shoe designs – she selected a royal blue shoe with a four-inch heel, which was then created for Kate in her size (five and a half). Designer Becka Hunt, who was inspired by the sapphire in Kate's engagement ring, said: 'I'm kind of in shock. It means everything.' Asked how William was, Kate admitted: 'I'm missing him desperately.' The Jubilee visit was not the first time that the royal family had visited Leicester: the Queen Mother opened Leicester College of Art's Fletcher Building in 1966 and the Monarch opened the eponymous Queens Building, which was home to the School of Engineering and Manufacture, on the campus in 1993.

Top: the Fiona Cairns bakery.
Above: De Monfort University.

LINCOLNSHIRE

GRIMSBY

Havelock Academy, Holyoake Rd, Grimsby, Lincolnshire DN32 8JH
National Fishing Heritage Centre, Alexandra Rd, Grimsby, Lincolnshire DN31 1UZ

The Duchess of Cambridge inadvertently sparked rumours that she was going to have a girl (obviously they were wrong) when she visited Grimsby four months before the birth of Prince George. During a walkabout outside the National Fishing Heritage Centre, a museum which depicts life as a trawler man in 1950s Britain, she was given a teddy bear by a member of the crowd, Diane Burton. Sandra Cook, who was standing next to her, was adamant that she heard her say: "Thank you. I will take that for my d..." before stopping herself. 'I leant over and said to her: "You were going to say daughter, weren't you?",' she revealed. She said: "No, we don't know." I said: "Oh, I think you do," to which she replied: "We're not telling." 'I only hope that she doesn't now give birth to a boy or I'm going to look pretty stupid,' she said. (her words have come back to haunt her). Afterwards Kate visited the Havelock Academy, where she opened its new building. The National Fishing Heritage Centre was set up in 1991 and depicts the history of the distant waters fishing fleet, as well as a range of temporary exhibitions. It won the Blue Peter Children's Museum of the Year award in 1993.

SLEAFORD

RAF Cranwell, Sleaford, Lincolnshire NG34 8HB

Top: Kate visits the National Fishing Heritage Centre. Above: Kate joined William for his graduation ceremony from the RAF's Central Flying School.

The market town of Sleaford is home to the RAF's Central Flying School, where Prince William spent four months in 2008 training to become a pilot. He was following in the footsteps of four generations of his family. His great-grandfather Prince Albert, later King George VI, was the first member of the royal family to serve in the RAF, immediately after its formation. Both Prince Philip and Prince Charles graduated as flight lieutenants, in 1953 and 1971 respectively, and, like William, Prince Charles received his wings from his father. Kate's family also have links to the RAF. Her grandfather Peter Middleton joined the service during the Second World War and got his wings in Canada. For the course, tailored specifically to his needs and intended to make him a competent rather than an operational flyer, William donned the RAF's instantly recognisable olive-green flying jumpsuit, with zips and name tag, to learn to fly solo and perform basic aerobatics. He was one of the first in his class at 1 Squadron of 1 Elementary Flying Training School to make a solo flight, eight days after his arrival, in a propeller-driven Grob G 115E light aircraft. Three months later, Kate joined Prince Charles and the Duchess of Cornwall for his graduation ceremony, smiling broadly as he received an insignia from his father. RAF Cranwell was commissioned on 1 April 1916 as a training college for the Royal Naval Air Service, which merged with the Army's Royal Flying Corps to form the RAF two years later. The Royal Air Force College opened in 1920 under the command of Air Commodore Sir Charles Longcroft. Fourteen years later, the future Edward VIII opened its current brick and Portland stone building, with its central portico of six Corinthian columns.

STOKE ROCHFORD

St Andrew and St Mary's Church Stoke Rochford, Lincolnshire NG33 5ED

Above: St Andrew and St Mary's Church.

St Andrew and St Mary's Church is notable for the wedding of William's cousin, Emily McCorquodale – the daughter of Princess Diana's sister Sarah, who beat cancer as a teenager – and film director James Hutt. The Duke and Duchess of Cambridge and Prince Harry attended the ceremony but their appearance was overshadowed when Sarah's uncle Earl Spencer arrived at the church hand-in-hand with his third wife Karen Gordon, who was pregnant with his seventh child. The church lies a stone's throw from Stoke Rochford Hall, a hotel and conference centre, designed by William Burn, which was the location for the drawing-up of plans for the Allies' unsuccessful military operation Market Garden in 1944. Members of the 2nd Battalion of the Parachute regiment meet annually at the church to remember their fallen.

NOTTINGHAMSHIRE

NOTTINGHAM

Council House, Old Market Square, Smithy Row, Nottingham NG1 2DT
Old Market Square, Nottingham NG1 2BY

The Queen's visit to the Midlands was her first official engagement in front of crowds since her Diamond Jubilee weekend in London – she was accompanied by the Duke and Duchess of Cambridge because the Duke of Edinburgh was recovering from a bladder infection. William and Kate, who arrived at Nottingham railway station ahead of her, greeted the Monarch as she got off the royal train. 'Are you waiting for the same train we are?' William joked to flag-waving passengers on the opposite side of the tracks. The royal party was attending a reception in 2012 for couples celebrating their diamond wedding anniversary at Nottingham's Council House. They walked through the heaving crowd in the town's Old Market Square, where Kate was presented with a posy by eight-year-old meningitis survivor Isabelle Weall. After waving from the balcony of the Council House (where Torvill and Dean greeted the crowds after their Olympic triumph) they went inside to meet couples such as Kaylet Smedley, 80, and her husband, 86. 'We've still got a long way to go,' William (married one year) told them. Nottingham's Old Market Square has been the centre of Nottingham life since it was founded by the 11th century Norman knight William Peveril, who lived in Nottingham Castle. Home to Nottingham's old market, it was the original setting for the annual Nottingham Goose Fair and the location of the earliest provincial bank in England, Smith's Bank (its successor the National Westminster Bank, is located in the same premises). Legend has it that it is also where outlaw Robin Hood won a coveted silver arrow in a contest with the Sheriff of Nottingham. When the Nottingham Exchange was demolished – and the new Council House was built and opened by the future Edward VIII with a gold key, which is still displayed on a wall plaque inside the building, the square was redesigned.

Above: William and Kate join The Queen on the balcony of Nottingham's Council House.

WEST MIDLANDS

BIRMINGHAM

Aston Villa Football Club, Villa Park, Trinity Road, Birmingham B6 6HE
Library of Birmingham, Centenary Square, Broad St, Birmingham B1 2ND
Summerfield Community Centre, Winson Green, Birmingham B18 4EJ
South & City College Birmingham, Fusion Centre, High Street, Deritend, Digbeth, Birmingham B5 6DY
St Basils, Carole Gething House, 62 Arthur Street, Birmingham B10 0NJ
St Basils, John Austin Court, 45 Sutherland Street, Aston, Birmingham B6 7PT

The home city of Aston Villa football club was always going to hold a special place in Prince William's heart as he is a long-term supporter. After the birth of Prince George, the President of the Football Association revealed that he was determined his son would inherit his love of the Villans. In a message, recorded to mark the FA's 150th anniversary, the prince (who hosted the first football match at Buckingham Palace in 2013 between two of England's oldest amateur clubs, Civil Service FC and Polytechnic FC) joked: 'When Villa thrash Man U at Villa Park, my son will be there.' However it was on a more serious note that he visited Birmingham for the first time with the Duchess of Cambridge. The couple met business and community leaders at Summerfield Community Centre, in the heart of Winson Green, which was torn apart during the 2011 riots. They also met parents of the three men, who died defending their community from looters - Haroon Jahan, 21, and brothers Shazad Ali, 30, and Abdul Musavir, 31. Two years later Prince William returned alone to Birmingham for a three-stop tour of the city. His first port of call was the Carole Gething House, a shelter run by St Basils' housing association, which was founded in 1972 as a night shelter for the homeless (known colloquially as 'The Boot') and now has spread across the city. As patron of Centrepoint, he wanted to discuss his End Youth Homelessness campaign. Joking about his rock star performance with Taylor Swift and Jon Bon Jovi, earlier that week, he said: 'I'm not doing that again.' He then travelled into the city centre to tour the newly-opened state-of-the-art Birmingham Library, where he took part in a children's reading group. His third – and final – engagement of the day was at South & City College, where he toured its Grade II listed Handsworth Campus, which was undergoing a £3 million restoration. There he met community groups, who had been working on building relations in the aftermath of the riots. William's third visit to Birmingham was to visit John Austin Court, another shelter run by the St Basil's homeless charity. He returned in 2014 to learn about their Mental Skills Training scheme – part of their BOOST programme, to help get youngsters back into work, watching a video of a residential trip and having a cup of tea (milk with one sugar).

Previous page: the ruins of Coventry Cathedral. Above left: Birmingham's state-of-the-art library. Left: William at South & City College.

COVENTRY

War Memorial Park, Kenilworth Rd, Coventry CV3 6PT

Coventry's War Memorial Park was the first of 500 parks, chosen by the charity the Fields in Trust and the Royal British Legion, to be protected in perpetuity as a 'centenary field' to mark the 100th anniversary of World War 1. Prince William, who is president of the charity, laid a wreath at the memorial in 2014 and unveiled a plaque, granting it special status. He then met Graham Williams, great-nephew of Royal Warwickshire Regiment officer Arthur Hutt ,who was the first person from Coventry to be awarded the Victoria Cross for his role during the Battle of Passchendaele. 'Each moment of play or use that takes place on a memorial field is, in a way, an act of remembrance,' he said. Afterwards, to prove his point, he demonstrated his tennis skills. Coventry's largest city park opened in 1921 as a tribute to the soldiers from the city who lost their lives in the Great War. Its 90ft War Memorial, which houses a Chamber of Silence, was built in 1927.

WALSALL

Walsall Gala Baths, Tower St, Walsall WS1 1DH

Above left: William lays a wreath at Coventry's War Memorial Park.
Above right: the prince greets the crowd in Coventry.

To the sound of the theme tune of Rocky, Prince William made his first visit to the Midlands for the Under 18s Water Polo Championships. William, who was patron of the English Schools' Swimming Association, officially 'dropped the ball' to start the 2008 tournament, between Bolton School and King Edward's School, Birmingham, at Walsall Gala Baths. He revealed, in the event programme, that he had been passionate about the sport since playing at Eton, representing Scotland in the university championships when he was at St Andrews. 'I have always been a keen supporter of water polo,' he wrote. 'These Championships provide a fantastic opportunity for boys and girls in secondary education throughout England to compete in teams to an exceptionally high standard. Taking part in ESSA events when I was at school provided me with the motivation and enthusiasm to go on later to represent Scottish Universities and the Army. Therefore, it gives me great pleasure to be here today, and to be able to share with you the enjoyment of such high quality water polo – a sport that is physically challenging and competitive, yet hugely rewarding.'

SHROPSHIRE

SHREWSBURY

RAF Shawbury, Shrewsbury, Shropshire SY4 4DZ

The Defence Helicopter Flying School at RAF Shawbury was where Prince William did an advanced helicopter training course in order to become an RAF search and rescue pilot (Prince Charles presented him with his flying badge in 2010). Flt Lt Wales, codenamed 'Golden Osprey', trained on a single-engine Squirrel helicopter before progressing to a Griffin, which has a winchman and crew. He and Prince Harry, who was also at the flying school, rented a country house in Shropshire, complete with swimming pool and tennis courts, instead of living in cramped rooms on the base. RAF Shawbury is housed on an airfield that was used for training in WWI - it was known as No 9 Training Depot Station, Royal Flying Corps - and WWII, which was home to No 11 Flying Training School and No 27 Maintenance Unit. Today Shawbury is home to two main training units – Central Air Traffic Control School and the tri-service Defence Helicopter Flying School.

Right: William at RAF Shawbury, where he undertook an advanced helicopter training course.

STAFFORDSHIRE

ALREWAS

National Memorial Arboretum, Croxhall Road, Alrewas, Staffordshire DE13 7AR

A memorial to the 1914 Christmas Day truce, designed by a ten-year-old schoolboy, whose great-great-grandfather was killed during World War I, was unveiled by the Duke of Cambridge at the National Memorial Arboretum to commemorate the centenary of the war. Prince William dedicated the sculpture 'Football Remembers' to those killed in the war, and praised Spencer Turner's 'stunning' design – a steel football with the clasped hands of an English and German soldier - as capturing 'the very essence of the Christmas Truce'. It was the second time that William had visited the Armed Forces Memorial: he launched the £12 million National Memorial Arboretum Future Foundations Appeal there in 2009. The National Memorial Arboretum, which has 50,000 trees, covering 150 acres, was the brainchild of Commander David Childs, a retired naval officer, who wanted a national place of remembrance for Britain's fallen heroes. It opened in 2001 and now has more than 300 memorials to the armed forces, emergency services and voluntary organisations.

BURTON ON TRENT

St George's Park, Newborough Road, Needwood, Burton on Trent, Staffordshire DE13 9PD

St George's Park is the home of Britain's £15 million National Football Centre, which was opened by Prince William, who is President of the Football Association, and the Duchess of Cambridge in 2012. The couple met England football manager Roy Hodgson and the squad at the ground, ahead of their World Cup qualification game against San Marino, and posed for a photograph with them. 'I feel tempted to cry: "God for Harry, England and St George," he joked, "but I really don't want to lower the tone by bringing my brother into it." Afterwards the prince made a beeline for Chelsea left back Ashley Cole, who had been charged with misconduct after allegedly calling the governing body a 'bunch of t***s' on Twitter over the John Terry racial abuse verdict. 'If you continue to be a naughty boy they will take away your Twitter account,' William is reported to have told him. Set in the National Forest, in 330 acres of landscaped parkland, the National Football Centre, which has a 228-bedroom Hilton Hotel, is the training base for the 24 England teams, as well as being the home of FA learning, its educational wing. It has 12 full-size pitches and an elite training pitch, which is an exact replica of Wembley.

Above: the National Memorial Arboretum.
Left: Kate at St George's Park, home of the National Football Centre.

ROCESTER

JCB World Headquarters, Rocester, Staffordshire ST14 5JP

When Prince William visited Rocester in 2009 he fulfilled every schoolboy's dream by driving a JCB. The prince was celebrating a milestone in the company's history by launching its 750,000th machine – a 3CX backhoe loader, which travels up to speeds of 60mph (the British Army has invested £7 million in a fleet for deployment in Afghanistan). Chairman Sir Anthony Bamford, who introduced William to his son Jo and daughter Alice, showed the prince JCB's first-ever product, a screw-tipping farm trailer, which was made by his father Joseph Bamford, who founded the company in a garage in Uttoxeter in 1945, and now stands in reception. JCB now has 22 plants on four continents. Its millionth JCB machine, a 22-tonne JS220 tracked excavator in shimmering silver rolled off the production line in 2013.

Left: William gets behind the wheel of a JCB at the company's headquarters.

WALES

WALES

BODORGAN

Bodorgan Estates, Bodorgan, Isle of Anglesey LL62 5LP

With a private beach and views of Snowdonia, a four-bedroom whitewashed farmhouse on the south west corner of the island is where the Duke and Duchess of Cambridge spent their first years of married life. William paid £750 a week to landowner Sir George Meyrick to rent the house near RAF Valley, when he began his search and rescue training in 2010, and openly shared the house with Kate (although she retained her London pied-à-terre for discretion). The couple led a simple life – although William's commute to work was out of the ordinary. He would leave at 6.45am each day in a black Range Rover followed by security or be collected by a Sea King search and rescue helicopter, which would land in the grounds of the estate.

They would regularly enjoy Wednesday night suppers of shepherd's pie and claret up at 'the big house' (the stately home, Bodorgan Hall, owned by the Meyricks), go pheasant shooting once a month and watch Downton Abbey on Sunday evenings (according to Jessica Brown Findlay, who played Lady Sybil Crawley, they were 'huge fans'). During the summer months, they would have barbecues on the beach – on one occasion Kate, who is a volunteer for the Scout Organisation, cooked burgers for local cubs and beaver scouts and helped them fish and catch crabs. 'My eight-year-old stepbrother went over to Kate Middleton's house for a BBQ,' one fan tweeted. 'I'm about to cry with jealousy.' Sometimes the couple would drive around in a battered white Ford Transit van, wearing baseball caps and sunglasses to remain incognito; at other times William would speed along the country lanes, dressed in leathers and a helmet, on his red and white 180mph Ducati motorbike, Kate occasionally riding pillion. The Bodorgan estate was given to one of Sir George Meyrick's ancestors by Henry VIII. The farmhouse, which is accessed by a private lane, is totally secluded.

Previous page: Llandwynn Beach.
Above: the remote Bodorgan estate.

CARDIFF

Llandaff Cathedral, Cathedral Close, Cardiff CF5 2LA
Millennium Stadium, Westgate Street, Cardiff CF10 1NS

As the son of the Prince of Wales, Prince William has an affinity with the Welsh capital. It was in Cardiff that he made his first public appearance with his parents: he attended a 1991 Thanksgiving service at the newly-restored 12th century Llandaff Cathedral, which contains a triptych by Daniel Gabriel Rossetti and a statue by Sir Jacob Epstein (after the service, he signed the visitors' book and revealed he was left-handed). Since then the Prince, who is vice-patron of the Welsh Rugby Union, has been a regular at the Millennium Stadium, cheering on Wales at the Six Nations' International and the Prince William Rugby Cup, which was created in 2007 to celebrate 100 years of rugby union history between Wales and South Africa. After the 2013 Wales South Africa match (Wales were beaten 24-15), he met artist Dan Llywelyn Hall, who had been commissioned by the Welsh Rugby Union to paint a portrait of the Queen for her 60th anniversary, and Welsh First Minister Carwyn Jones, who gave him a certificate for Prince George from the initiative Plant!, which sows a tree for every child born (or adopted) in Wales. He has also taken Kate to watch the rugby and meet beneficiaries of the Welsh Rugby Charitable Trust, of which he is patron. In 2014 William was given a charity calendar, featuring female players in the nude, and said, enthusiastically: 'Very good shots. I can recommend this.' Kate was out of earshot at the time, having tea with former players.

Top: the 12th century Llandaff Cathedral.

HOLYHEAD

Breakwater Country Park, Holyhead, Isle of Anglesey LL65 1YG
Empire Cinema 39 Stanley Street, Holyhead, Isle of Anglesey LL65 1HL
RAF Valley, Holyhead, Isle of Anglesey LL65 3NY
The Showground, Gwalchmai, Holyhead, Isle of Anglesey LL65 4RW

William's first stint at RAF Valley was in the run-up to his time at Sandhurst: he spent two weeks doing 'work experience' with the Mountain Rescue Team in 2005, learning emergency lifesaving skills and taking part in a mock rescue, abseiling down a 200ft cliff while holding one end of a stretcher (filled with ballast to simulate an injured climber). While there, he sparked controversy when he was flown on a Hawk jet to RAF Lyneham, to collect the army boots he wanted to break in for Sandhurst. He returned to Anglesey four years later to train as a search and rescue pilot on its famous yellow Sea King helicopters – he qualified in 2010 and signed a three-year contract. 'I now want to build on the experience and training I have received to serve operationally,' he said at the time. 'For good reasons, I was not able to deploy to Afghanistan this year with D Squadron of the Household Cavalry Regiment. The time I spent with the RAF earlier this year made me realise how much I love flying. Joining Search and Rescue is a perfect opportunity for me to serve in the forces operationally, while contributing to a vital part of the country's emergency services'. During his time at RAF Valley, William was on call for 24-hour shifts, playing the computer game Call of Duty with crewmates (when not dealing with an emergency) and enjoying a pint with fellow officers at the pub after his shift. When he was not at work, William was often spotted in Holyhead going to the Empire Cinema with Kate (they wore Day-Glo comedy afro wigs on a 'team jolly' to Toy Story 3) visiting the Anglesey Show, where he chatted to young farmers and watched gundog and falconry displays and starting the Ring O' Fire Anglesey Coastal Ultra Marathon, at Holyhead Breakwater Country Park (Kate made a surprise appearance weeks after the birth of Prince George).

Above: William at the controls of the famous yellow search and rescue Sea King.
Right: William learns about falconry at the Anglesey Show.

LLANDDWYN BEACH

Llanddwyn Beach, Isle of Anglesey LL61 6SG

The Duke and Duchess of Cambridge were often spotted walking their dog Lupo on Llanddwyn Beach when they lived in Anglesey. The couple would walk hand in hand along the five-mile stretch of beach (Llanddwyn is named after St Dwynwen, who is the Welsh patron saint of lovers). The beach, which is backed by forest and extensive dunes at the south-west tip of Anglesey, has views of Snowdonia National Park, and a path leading to Llanddwyn Island nature reserve.

LLANDUDNO

St Dunstan's Centre, Queens Road, Llandudno, Conwy LL30 1UT
Cineworld, Junction Leisure Park, Off Junction Way, Llandudno Junction, Conwy LL31 9XX

When Prince William first arrived on the island of Anglesey in 2010 he paid a visit to Llandudno to see the St Dunstan's Centre for blind ex-servicemen and women. He is the first royal to have visited the centre, which opened the following year, although the royal family has been involved with the charity Blind Veterans UK since it was launched after World War I (Princess Alexandra was its first patron). During his visit William met Simon Brown, who was blinded by sniper fire in Iraq (he showed him his glass eye with a Union Jack printed on it) and tried his hand at archery under the instruction of former Welsh guardsman Clive Jones, who lost his sight in both eyes when he was assaulted while off duty (William was blindfolded). 'I'm sure he'll make a good shot with practice,' Jones joked. Blind Veterans UK was set up by Sir Arthur Pearson, then President of the Royal National Institute for the Blind, who had lost his own sight through glaucoma. In 1996, one of its members, Don Planner became the first blind man to climb Mont Blanc. William and Kate were also regulars at Llandudno's Cineworld cinema, watching the latest release. They were spotted in a screening of the American comedy Bridesmaids, roared with laughter at the Inbetweeners and watched the James Bond film Skyfall (they bought two drinks and a large box of popcorn).

Top: Llanddwyn Beach, where William and Kate often walked their dog Lupo. Left: William tries his hand at blind archery.

LLANTRISANT

Royal Mint, Llantrisant, Pontyclun, Rhondda Cynon Taf CF72 8YT

The birth of Prince George marked a special day for the Royal Mint – they struck 2,013 'lucky' silver pennies for children born on the same day as the Duke and Duchess of Cambridge's first child. It was the first time that a coin had been struck by the Mint to mark a royal birth. The commemorative coin was worth £28 but parents obtained one free by registering their child's birth on the Royal Mint's Facebook site. Each penny, which was dated 2013, featured a shield of the Royal Arms, and was sent out in a blue or pink purse (depending on the sex of the child). Enclosed was a card, decorated with a teddy bear, and bearing the words: 'Solid sterling silver good luck penny.' The Royal Mint also produced 10,000 sterling silver crown-sized £5 coins (costing £80) and 2,013 22-carat gold sovereigns (£800), using an 1817 design of St George slaying the dragon by the artist Benedetto Pistrucci. 'It was always going to be George and the dragon as the symbol of England,' a spokesman said. 'It was a very happy coincidence.' Nobody knows on what day the Royal Mint was founded but, by the second half of the 9th century, coins were in general circulation. By 1270, the monarch's mint was based in the Tower of London.

MENAI BRIDGE

Waitrose, Mona Road, Menai Bridge, Isle of Anglesey LL59 5EA

Waitrose in Menai Bridge is now the most famous supermarket in Britain. The Duchess of Cambridge regularly shopped there when she was living in Anglesey - she was snapped there just days after the royal wedding pushing her trolley down the aisle, with her protection officer lagging behind.

MERTHYR TYDFIL

Central Beacons Mountain Rescue, High Street, Dowlais, Merthyr Tydfil, Vale of Glamorgan CF48 3PW

Prince William met one of his oldest fans in Merthyr Tydfil in 2008 when he spent the afternoon with the Central Beacons Mountain Rescue team. Ivy Evans, 92, had met his great-great grandmother Queen Mary when she was in service in London. 'I'm in my working clothes,' she said. 'I was just in the house cooking chips. I didn't know I was coming over. He was lovely. He made my day.' William, who is patron of Mountain Rescue Council England and Wales, was in the Brecon Beacons to do a practice rescue operation with the team, one of four civilian mountain rescue teams, which cover the Beacons' National Park. Its patch includes Pen Y Fan, the highest point in Southern Britain, at 886m and the valley of Ystradfellte waterfalls. After switching from a suit, to trainers and a helmet, William lowered a man on a stretcher as part of the mock rescue.

Above: the Royal Mint in Llantrisant. Left: William meets members of the Central Beacons Mountain Rescue team.

PEMBROKE

The Valero Pembroke Refinery, Pembroke, Pembrokeshire SA71 5SJ

The Duke and Duchess of Cambridge created their own brand of gasoline in 2014 when they visited the Valero Pembroke oil refinery to celebrate its 50th anniversary. The couple met with some of the 1,500 workers at the refinery, which was opened by the Queen Mother in 1964, before travelling in a minibus to one of three control rooms on the 1,270-acre site. 'Nicely spruced up for our arrival,' joked William, as they walked into the room. 'I can smell the paint.' After being invited to press a button to create their own gasoline, Kate, who was 15 weeks pregnant, turned to William and said: 'Shall I do one and you can do the other one?' She pressed the button and William quipped: 'We are waiting for the red light to go off.' After pressing his own button (the group clapped loudly) he was informed it would take 15 hours to blend. 'We will do the night shift,' he joked. The couple left Prince George at home but he was not forgotten – when they left, workers gave them a plastic model of a fuel tanker, complete with the number plate 4 GEORGE (they gave a similar gift to the Queen Mother for a young Prince Andrew in 1964). Built in a deep natural harbour at Rhoscrowther, the Pembroke Refinery supplies 10 per cent of the UK's fuel: it processes 270,000 barrels a day and has a pipeline stretching as far as Manchester.

RHOSCOLYN

White Eagle Pub, Rhoscolyn, Isle of Anglesey LL65 2NJ

This gastro-pub, opened in 2007, became one of the Duke and Duchess' favourite pubs when they were living on Anglesey. The couple would pop in for its £12.50 'Snowdon' burger.

RHOSNEIGR

Funsport, 1 Beach Terrace, Rhosneigr, Isle of Anglesey LL64 5QB
Gecko Clothes, High Street, Rhosneigr, Isle of Anglesey LL64 5UQ

Top: William and Kate visit the Valero Pembroke Oil Refinery to help mark its 50th anniversary. Above: the White Eagle Pub.

She may be one of the most famous women in the world – but when the Duchess of Cambridge popped into Funsport, owner Dave Buckland failed to recognise her. Kate dropped into the shop to buy a wetsuit but had forgotten her wallet so she asked if she could reserve it and pop back later. Dave, known locally as Bucky, was happy to do so but asked for her name. 'Mrs Cambridge,' she replied. Even then he didn't twig - he even commented that she had an unusual surname. Kate has also been shopping at Gecko Clothes, a clothing and accessory store in the hamlet, where she bought cushions. Rhosneigr, which has a population of 745, has become a magnet for tourists as its sandy beach is one of the best spots in the UK for windsurfing and surfing.

TONYPANDY

Dinas Community and Family Hub, Flat 54, Pen Dinas, Porth, Tonypandy, Rhondda Cynon Taff CF40 1JD
Soar Centre, Tylacelyn Road, Penygraig, Tonypandy , Rhondda, Cynon Taff CF40 1JZ

Aston Villa supporter Prince William pledged to wear a Cardiff City pin badge for the 2008 FA Cup final when he made his first official visit to the South Wales valleys. William was given the badge by Cardiff fan Duane Price, one of a crowd of schoolchildren, waiting patiently in the sunshine, outside the Soar Centre, run by the charity Valley Kids and based in a former Baptist chapel (Cardiff lost 1-0 to Portsmouth). It was William's second stop of the day to see first-hand the charity's work with disadvantaged children and their families (he was invited after watching the Valley Kids perform at his Prince William Cup the previous year). Earlier in the day he visited the charity's project in Pen Dinas, where he watched a performance of break-dancing and played a game of Wii tennis. 'You know you're not allowed to beat me,' he joked to his 18-year-old opponent Martyn James. When the teenager lost, he said: 'I was stitched up.' Valley Kids opened the Soar Centre in 1987 to work in one of the most deprived areas of Europe. Its new £800,000 arts and community centre was funded by the Arts Council of Wales.

TREARDDUR BAY

Lifeboat Station, Fron Towyn, Lon Isallt, Trearddur Bay, Isle of Anglesey LL65 2UL
Trearddur Bay Hotel, Trearddur Bay, Isle of Anglesey LL65 2UN

The village of Trearddur Bay marked a milestone in the life of the Duchess of Cambridge – it was where she made her first public appearance and her formal debut on the island she was to call home. She and Prince William were attending the naming ceremony and service of dedication of the Atlantic 85 inflatable 'Hereford Endeavour' at the village's lifeboat station. The couple sang along to the Welsh national anthem, before pouring champagne over the bow of the vessel. When veteran royalist Colin Edwards brandished a photograph of William and Harry with Princess Diana, she grabbed it and pointed saying: 'Oh my goodness. Look at his knees.' The couple have returned to the bay on many occasions since they got married – dining at the Trearddur Bay Hotel. The RNLI established their first inshore lifeboat station in the village in 1967 – it was equipped with a D-class lifeboat.

Left: Kate makes her first public appearance.

YORKSHIRE & THE HUMBER

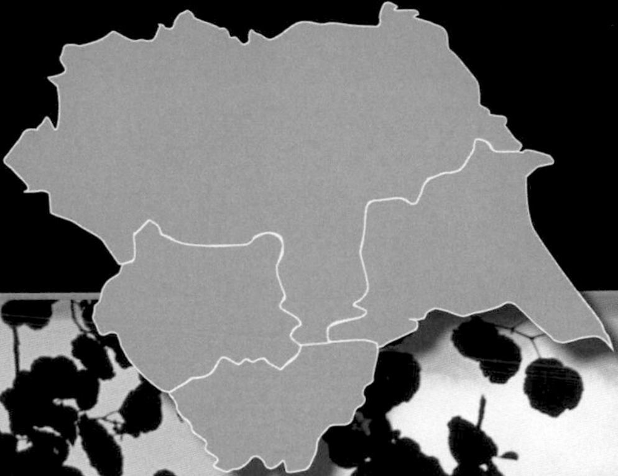

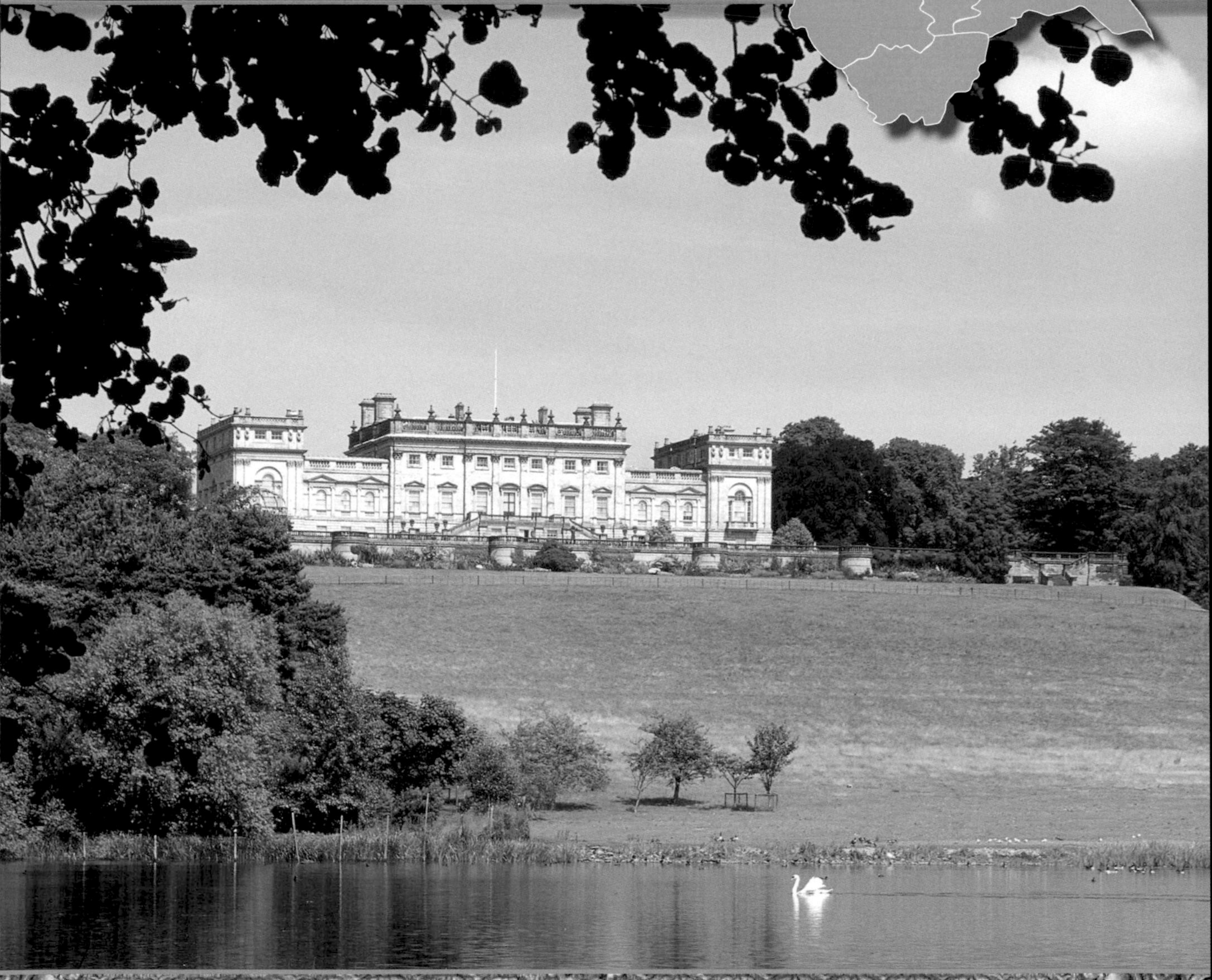

EAST RIDING OF YORKSHIRE

GOOLE

Goole Academy, Centenary Road, Goole, East Riding of Yorkshire DN14 6AN

Prince William's trip to Goole was to launch his Junior Prince's Award - a national award for underprivileged primary school children to motivate them to achieve at school and help their transition from primary to secondary school. William, who is patron of SkillForce, which harnesses the talents of former military personnel to inspire the youngsters, launched the award at Goole Academy to celebrate the charity's 10th anniversary. The Prince met teachers and pupils at the school and saw how the charity's instructors used practical, hands-on games, tasks and challenges to engage pupils such as a D-Day bridge building exercise. Chatting to the pupils, he revealed that he was a fan of Coldplay – and had tasted Morrisons Value pasta ('not bad' was his verdict). However he refused an offer to play drums with the school's samba band, saying: 'I used to play the piano, trumpet and drums when I was your age but I couldn't read music. There's only so much you can remember from the top of your head.' The Junior Prince's Award, which involves team building and problem-solving challenges, such as remembrance and respect; team sports; outdoor pursuits (including camping out for a night); first aid; navigation; and a Social Action Project (working in the community to benefit others). Students complete a log book to reflect on what they have learnt and receive a SkillForce certificate and programme.

Previous page: Harewood House.
Top: William arrives at Goole Academy.

KINGSTON UPON HULL

Associated British Ports, Port House, Northern Gate, Kingston Upon Hull, East Riding of Yorkshire HU9 5PQ
Humberside Fire and Rescue Service Headquarters, Summergroves Way, Kingston Upon Hull, East Riding of Yorkshire HU4 7BB

Kingston Upon Hull (known colloquially as Hull) is the home port of HMS Iron Duke, where Prince William spent five weeks out at sea – it was the longest that he had been apart from the Duchess of Cambridge (at that stage) since they began dating at St Andrews University. The prince embarked on the Type 23 frigate, a 4,900-ton warship that was working with American Drug Enforcement Administration agents to track down cocaine smugglers during the hurricane season in the Caribbean, during the summer of 2008. After just four days on the warship, armed US coastguards seized £40 million-worth of cocaine from a speedboat north-east of Barbados. William was on board the Lynx helicopter that spotted the 50ft vessel and apparently played a key 'planning and surveillance' role in the seizure. Later, he took part in a hurricane disaster training exercise off the volcanic island of Montserrat, as one of the forward command team landing on the island. Iron Duke, the third ship to bear its name, was launched in 1991 by Lady King in the presence of the Duke and Duchess of Wellington. It was named after their ancestor Arthur Wellesley, 1st Duke of Wellington, who was known as the 'Iron Duke'. Her motto 'Virtutis Fortuna Comes' (Fortune is the Companion of Valour), is inherited from the Duke of Wellington's 33rd Regiment of Foot. Hull is also where the Duchess of Cambridge paid a visit four months before she became a mother. She visited Humberside Fire and Rescue Services, where Claire Moss-Smith, 86, a patient at a local hospice, told her: 'I'm waiting for you to be Queen.' 'You might be waiting for a long time,' she smiled.

Above: HMS Iron Duke.

North Yorkshire

Aldborough

St Andrew's Church, Aldborough, York, North Yorkshire YO51 9EY
The Ship Inn, Low Road, Aldborough, York, North Yorkshire YO51 9ER

The 2011 wedding of Harry Aubrey-Fletcher, son of the Lord Lieutenant of Buckingham-shire, and Louise Stourton, daughter of the 24th Baron Stourton, was the first wedding that the Duke and Duchess of Cambridge attended after announcing their engagement. William was an usher at the ceremony, which took place the day before Kate's 29th birthday, and Prince Harry and Princess Beatrice were among the guests at St Andrew's parish church – the princes had known Harry, who works in mergers and acquisitions at JP Morgan, since he was at Ludgrove prep school and he and William were both members of the Eton Society. The main wedding party arrived in a vintage bus but Kate (who unusually was wearing black) turned up in a chauffeur-driven Range Rover, with her security detail. While most of the guests sipped mulled wine in the church before the service, the groom and ushers slipped away for a wedding breakfast at the local pub, the Ship Inn (William had cottage pie). Land-lords Brian and Elaine Rey are old hands at serving royalty – when they ran their first pub, the Fox & Hounds, near RAF Leeming, Prince Andrew was a regular (Gordon Ramsay is also a fan of their Traditional Sunday Roast, hence their Campaign for Real Gravy). After the ceremony William and Harry left in Audi A5s, while Kate and Beatrice took the bus to the reception at Louise's family seat Castle Allerton. The 14th century St Andrew's Church is the third church to occupy what is believed to be the site of a Roman Temple of Mercury – it was rebuilt after the previous church was partially destroyed by Scots raiders in 1318.

Allerton Mauleverer

Allerton Park Mansion, Allerton Park, Allerton Mauleverer, North Yorkshire HG5 0SE

Top: the 14th century St Andrew's Church. Above: A birds' eye view of Allerton Park Castle.

Allerton Park was the venue of the wedding reception of Harry Aubrey-Fletcher and Louise Stourton, eldest daughter of Edward Stourton, 24th Baron Stourton, and distant cousin of former Radio 4 Today presenter Ed Stourton. The couple threw a party in a marquee in its grounds for guests including the Duke and Duchess of Cambridge. Next door to the park lies England's 'grandest and most elegant gothic revival stately home' Allerton Castle, setting for the film The Secret Garden and TV series Sherlock Holmes. It was once owned by the Stourton family but now belongs to a charitable trust. Charles Stourton, 17th Baron Stourton, bought the land and its original Georgian mansion for £153,315 in 1805 from Prince Frederick, Duke of York and brother of King George IV, and rechristened it 'Stourton Towers'. However, later that century Charles Stourton, 19th Baron, demolished the mansion and built the current castle - only one wing of the original survives.

HARROGATE

West Park, Harrogate, North Yorkshire HG1 1BJ

There was much anticipation in Harrogate on the opening day of the Tour de France as it is the hometown of Mark Cavendish's mother Adele. However the cyclist crashed in the final sprint to the finish line, dislocating his collar bone, and the Duke and Duchess of Cambridge presented German cyclist, Marcel Kittel, who won the first stage of the 2,277-mile three week-race to Paris, with the yellow jersey.

YORK

RAF Linton-on-Ouse, York, North Yorkshire YO30 2AL

Top: William and Kate at the Tour de France, Harrogate. Above: William at the controls of a Tucano T1 helicopter at RAF Linton-On-Ouse.

Linton-on-Ouse was Prince William's home after he left the Central Flying School at RAF Cranwell. He arrived there in 2008 to be trained on the Tucano T1, which can fly at speeds of up to 345 mph. There he did a tailor-made course designed to develop skills such as general aircraft handling, formation flying and low-level navigation. RAF Linton-on-Ouse was one of around 50 RAF stations constructed in the run-up to World War II, as part of its rapid response to German rearmament. During the war it was home to Headquarters No 4 (Bomber) Group, which was commanded by Air Commodore Harris, later Commander-in-Chief of Bomber Command. Today it provides fast-jet pilot training for Royal Navy, RAF, Foreign and Commonwealth students in preparation for advanced training on the Hawk at RAF Valley, as well as refresher and instructor training for qualified RAF and Royal Navy pilots.

SOUTH YORKSHIRE

ROTHERHAM

Healthbeds, Kingsforth Road, Thurcroft Industrial Estate, Rotherham, South Yorkshire S66 9HU

Above: left to right, Healthbeds owner David Smeaton, his grandfather Harry Smeaton, who founded the company, and father Tony Smeaton.

The town of Rotherham has the distinction of being the place where the Duke and Duchess of Cambridge bought their marital bed. Kate tracked down family firm Healthbeds and ordered an exact replica of the model the couple slept in at their farmhouse in Anglesey. The company, which was founded in 1893 by Arthur Smeaton, then made a bespoke mattress (to fit a four-poster bed), with 4,200 springs, made of 'sumptuous cashmere, silk, cotton and wool fillings'. Arthur's grandson David, who now runs the company, said: 'We got a call out of the blue from one of the Duchess's staff asking if we could provide one like the model they slept in. The Duchess loved the bed so much, apparently she looked under the mattress to find a label to discover where it was made. We are thrilled to have royalty buying one of our beds. I think it's the first time.' Healthbeds is a founder member of the Sleep Council and a member of the Guild of Master Craftsmen.

WEST YORKSHIRE

LEEDS

Harewood House, Harewood, Leeds, West Yorkshire LS17 9LG

Above: Harewood House.

2014 was the year the Tour de France came to Yorkshire and the Grade I listed Harewood House – one of the Treasure Houses in England – proved the perfect setting for its ceremonial start. After a spectacular Red Arrows display, and a rendition of the French and British national anthems, performed by the Band of the Corps of Royal Engineers, the Duchess of Cambridge, accompanied by Princes William and Harry, chatted to the British reigning champion of the Tour de France Chris Frome and sprinter Mark Cavendish, Britain's most successful Tour de France rider, before cutting the ribbon for the official start of the 101st

Above: Harewood House's extensive library, complete with furniture by Thomas Chippendale. Above right: its formal gardens, designed and laid by Capability Brown.

Tour. The 18th century house, which is owned by the Earl and Countess of Harewood, has been the family seat of the Lascelles family since its foundation stone was laid in 1759. King George VI's sister Princess Mary (the Queen's aunt and Lord Harewood's grandmother) married into the Lascelles family and lived at Harewood House until her death in 1965. It is a Georgian treasure: designed by architect John Carr, its lavish interiors were created by Robert Adam (who designed Whitehall's Admiralty Arch); its furniture is by Thomas Chippendale (it cost more than £10,000 in 1797); its grounds were laid out by Capability Brown and its terrace (planted yellow in the year of the Tour) was designed by Sir Charles Barry, architect of the House of Lords.

NORTH EAST

NORTHUMBERLAND
ALNWICK

Saint Michael - Alnwick
Northumberland

St Michael's Church, Bailiffgate, Alnwick, Northumberland NE66 1LY
Alnwick Castle, Alnwick, Northumberland NE66 1NQ

This handsome Grade I listed 15th century church was the venue of the 2013 wedding of William's old friend Thomas van Straubenzee (known as Van) and Lady Melissa Percy, daughter of the Duke and Duchess of Northumberland (Missy) who live in nearby Alnwick Castle. But it became known for the 'Battle of the Blondes'. It was the first meeting of Harry's two loves Chelsy Davy, who is Missy's best friend and was maid of honour, and Cressida Bonas, who was then dating Harry. Prince William, who has known Van since they were at Ludgrove prep school was joint best man while Prince Harry was an usher. The Duchess of Cambridge, who was heavily pregnant, remained at home but her sister Pippa Middleton was a guest. The bride, who was followed down the aisle by flower boys and girls, clad like fairies and pixies in green, wore a Bruce Oldfield dress. St Michael's Church was built on the site of a 12th century Norman chapel and its perpendicular structure is one of the architectural gems of Northumberland – it is included in England's 'Thousand Best Churches'. Its stained glass windows were described by art historian Nikolaus Pevsner as 'an uncommonly complete and enlightening survey of 19th century glass'. Visitors should observe its south east turret, which was used as a lookout to warn of raiders during the border conflicts. After the wedding Missy, who teaches tennis at the Queen's Club, in west London, and Van, who runs the estate agency VanHan, held their reception at Alnwick Castle, the family seat of the Northumberlands and home of Hogwarts School of Witchcraft and Wizardry and Downton Abbey's Brancaster Castle (the castle is often used as a film location). The couple greeted guests in the State Rooms of the castle before retiring to a marquee for dancing and fireworks. Alnwick Castle has towered over the village of Alnwick for more than 1,000 years. Bought by the Percy family 700 years ago, its famous Octagonal Towers at the entrance to the keep are rumoured to have been built with ransom money won by the 2nd Lord Percy after the Battle of Neville's Cross in 1346. There are 13 stone shields on the towers, representing families who have occupied the castle – or married into the Percy family – and the royal arms can be seen between the two towers.

Previous page: Alnwick Castle.
Above right: a drawing of St Michael's Church by the late Reverend Denis Sweetman, a talented clergyman, whose trademark signature included a figure of a monk.

TEESIDE

STOCKTON-ON-TEES

CRI Stockton Recovery Service, 17-18 High Street, Stockton-on-Tees, Teeside TS18 1SP

The Duchess of Cambridge won over hearts in Stockton-on-Tees as she patiently made her way down the line of people waiting behind barriers to greet her. Kate, who is patron of the charity Action on Addiction, was in the market town in 2012 visiting the CRI Stockton Recovery Centre, which works with families affected by drug and substance abuse. There she met parents and children involved in Action on Addiction's Moving Parents and Children Together (M-PACT) programme, which works with children whose parents are addicts. Stockton Recovery Service offers people who are trying to give up drugs and alcohol a holistic package of support to ensure they have a chance of recovery.

Right: Kate receives a posy as she visits the CRI Stockton Recovery Service.

TYNE AND WEAR

GATESHEAD

Gateshead Youth Council, 12 Gladstone Terrace, Gateshead, Tyne and Wear NE8 4DY

Above: Yummy Mummys at The Key.

When Kate paid a solo visit to the North East in 2012, after William dropped out at the last minute to go to the funeral of his nanny Olga Powell, she dropped into Gateshead Youth Council, to meet supporters of The Key, a charity which aims to unlock young people's true potential. There she met three kayakers, who paddled anti-clockwise around the UK, six friends who designed and created a sculpture and five teenagers, who created the Yummy Mummy's support network for other young mums. The Key was one of the organisations chosen by William and Kate to benefit from their Royal Wedding Charitable Gift Fund.

HETTON-LE-HOLE

6 Station Road, Hetton-Le-Hole, Houghton-Le-Spring, Tyne and Wear DH5 0AX

The pit village of Hetton-Le-Hole was the birthplace of the Duchess of Cambridge's grandmother Dorothy – and was the home of her ancestors. Kate's great-great-great-grandfather, John Harrison, migrated to the town in the 19th century and worked at Hetton Colliery. Barrington Terrace, which has long since been demolished, became the family home – it witnessed the birth of Kate's great-great grandfather John in 1874 and the death of his mother Jane from tuberculosis, seven years later, at the age of 42, leaving her husband, a widower, with ten children between the ages of two and 21. By 1890, tuberculosis (which in those days had no treatment) had cut a swathe through the family, killing his 18-year-old daughter Isabella. Grief-stricken at losing both his wife and daughter, he succumbed to the disease in 1889, having probably caught it at his daughter's bedside (his 17-year-old son James was the fourth victim the following year). Used to hardship (he was 14 when he became an orphan), Kate's great-great grandfather John, worked his way up to become a deputy at Lyons Colliery and married his wife, also called Jane. They too lived in Barrington Terrace, where they brought up their seven children, including Kate's great-grandfather Thomas. However John's career in the mines was cut tragically short when he was trampled by a runaway pony pulling a coal truck. After lying flat on his back for months, he was forced to give up work, spending the remainder of his life in considerable pain, supported by walking sticks. The couple moved to Broomhill Terrace after John retired but it, too, has been demolished. While three of Tommy's brothers moved down to London, he remained in the North East, working as a house joiner and living in Station Road. He married his wife Lily, mother of a daughter Ruth, in 1934, and Kate's grandmother Dorothy was born the following year. During the war Tommy served in Malaya but when he returned to Britain, he was off to London, setting in train the journey which would lead his great-granddaughter to the throne.

Top: the former Harrison family home, 7 Barrington Terrace. Middle: Kate's great-great grandparents John and Jane Harrison outside their home, 3 Broomhill Terrace. Above: Kate's great-great grandparents John and Jane Harrison

Above left: Kate's great-great grandparents John and Jane Harrison surrounded by their children c 1920. Left to right; Back row, Ernie, Jenny, Wilf, Jack; Middle Row, Kate's great-grandfather Thomas, John, Jane, Norman, Gladys, Front row; Twins George and Albert. Above right: Kate's great-great grandparents John and Jane Harrison.

NEWCASTLE UPON TYNE

Elswick Park, Elswick Road, Newcastle upon Tyne NE4 6SQ
Newcastle Civic Centre, Newcastle upon Tyne NE1 8QH
West Gate Community College Centre for Sport, West Road, Newcastle upon Tyne NE4 9L

Both the Duke and Duchess have visited Newcastle – but on different occasions after Prince William was forced to pull out of a second visit because of his nanny's funeral. During his first visit in 2007, Prince William caused a sensation – showing off his footballing skills and admitting that he would have liked to have been a professional footballer. William, who is president of the Football Association, was visiting West Gate Community College Centre for Sport to meet youngsters turning their lives around through the game. The Hat-Trick project, which is funded by UEFA, has been set up in 19 communities across the country since it was launched in 2005. After chatting to primary school children about 'fair play' ('He told me football is his favourite sport,' said Naseem Haque, who revealed that William wanted to be a footballer), he met teenagers, who have gained their Level 1 coaching qualification with funding from the FA and BBC Sport Relief. Finally (wearing one red sock for Sports Relief and one Eton Sock), he joined in a warm-up session with pupils from West Gate Community College before presenting a 'Fair Play' award to the winner of the five-a-side junior tournament. Kate toured Newcastle five years later on her own, after William had to pull out at the last-minute. Her first port of call was the Grade II listed Newcastle Civic Centre, which was designed by architect George Kenyon and opened by King Olav V of Norway in 1968 (US President Jimmy Carter delivered a speech there famously attempting the Geordie phrase 'Howay the lads'). On her arrival at the centre, she threw protocol to the wind and hugged ten-year-old Terry Campbell, who had travelled with his school to see the Duchess. He held out his arms and Kate said: 'Am I going to get a cuddle as well?' 'I was hoping to get a hug when we came here,' he said afterwards. 'I never actually thought it would happen. I can't believe she hugged me back.' Afterwards Kate visited a community garden in Elswick Park, which is protected under the Queen Elizabeth II Fields Challenge, of which William was patron (he is now President of Fields in Trust), and let slip that she grows her own potatoes (she only got small ones that year).

Above: Kate at Newcastle Civic Centre.
Opposite: Kate visits a community garden in Elswick Park.

SOUTH SHIELDS

Haven Point Leisure Centre, Pier Parade, South Shields, Tyne and Wear NE33 2JS

Above: William meets children at the Haven Point Leisure Centre.

Prince William made waves when he visited South Shields in 2013 to open its new £16 million swimming pool. Crowds of people waving flags gathered outside the Haven Point Leisure Centre, where he unveiled a commemorative plaque and signed the visitors' book. Members of South Tyneside Swimming Club and the English School's Swimming Association, of which William is patron, demonstrated their skills in the water and the prince met local Paralympic champions Josef Craig and Nicole Lough, who was its first customer when the centre opened its doors. Josef was Team GB's youngest swimming gold medallist in the 2012 Paralympic Games (the double world champion was crowned BBC Young Sports Personality of the Year and was awarded an MBE) and Nicole claimed bronze in swimming at the International Paralympic Committee World Swimming Championships in 2013. William then visited a workshop for young people taking part in the Diana Award – the only charity which bears his mother's name - joining in a parachute game and signing their anti-bullying wall. Haven Point, which has a life-sized wire mesh model of a man swimming butterfly suspended from its ceiling, has three pools, two dance studios, a gym, sauna and steam room.

NORTH WEST

CHESHIRE

CHESTER

Chester Cathedral, St Werburgh St, Chester CH1 2DY

The Duchess of Cambridge's absence from the 2004 wedding of Prince William's close friend Edward van Cutsem and the Duke of Westminster's daughter Lady Tamara Grosvenor in Chester Cathedral sparked speculation about the state of the royal relationship. But that was overshadowed by another absent guest: although the Queen and Prince Philip both attended the society wedding, Edward's godfather Prince Charles declined the invitation as he was visiting the families of soldiers serving with the Black Watch in Iraq. Rumours snowballed that the prince had boycotted the event after his consort, Camilla Parker Bowles, was not included in the royal party – she was reported to have been seated several rows

behind Charles and was expected to walk through a side entrance rather than the West Gate with other VIPs (Natalia, Duchess of Westminster, compared the seating plan to 'wading through treacle'). However both William and Harry, who are close friends of the four van Cutsem brothers – Edward, Hugh, Nicholas, and William – agreed to be ushers, wearing tails and pink rosebuds in their buttonholes, and the ceremony went off without a hitch. Afterwards the royal party attended the reception at the Duke of Westminster's country pile Eaton Hall, set in formal gardens a mile south of Eccleston, watching the stunning fireworks display and dining on scallops and prawns, fillet of beef and petits fours. The history of Chester Cathedral spans almost 2,000 years – according to legend both a prehistoric Druid temple and a Roman temple dedicated to Apollo existed on its site. The cathedral is housed in a former monastery built by the Earl of Chester, Hugh Lupus, nephew of William the Conqueror. Anselm, Abbot of Bec in Normandy, agreed to travel to Chester to establish the foundation of the church, which was built in the Romanesque style, in 1092. However by the time the cloisters and Chapter House had been constructed, in the mid 13th century, the original church looked old-fashioned and the monks decided to rebuild it in the Gothic style. The monastery was dissolved by Henry VIII in 1539 – however the King handed the monastery to the newly-created Diocese of Chester and the last Abbot became the first Dean of the cathedral. The cathedral has the only remaining ecclesiastical court in the country. Eaton Hall has been the country estate of the Grosvenor family since the 15th century and its main house has been rebuilt to match the architectural fashions of the age. The current house was built by Robert Grosvenor, 5th Duke of Westminster, in 1967 and cost £459,000 – the equivalent of £4.84 million today – but, after accusations that it was unsympathetic to its surroundings, it was refaced in a French classical style.

Previous page: The Lake District.
Above: the Romanesque Chester Cathedral.

CUMBRIA

BARROW-IN-FURNESS

BAE Systems, Bridge Road Barrow-in-Furness, Cumbria LA14 1AF

It is not the kind of job where you bump into old friends. But, when the Duchess of Cambridge paid a royal visit to Britain's only submarine builders, in Barrow-in-Furness, she came face to face with someone she knew from childhood. Prince William, who is Commodore-in-Chief of the Royal Navy Submarine Service, was visiting BAE Systems with Kate, who was six

months pregnant, to officially open its Future Submarines Office. There she met quality inspector Matthew Lidiard, whose parents knew the Middletons when they were growing up in Berkshire. The couple also met crew members of the submarine Artful and were given a baby grow for their forthcoming arrival (Prince George). As they left, William who was given a mounted submarine section of pressure hull welding, quipped: 'You can get back to work now. Your tea break is over.'

GLENRIDDING

The Raven, Ullswater Steamers, The Pier House, Glenridding, Cumbria CA11 0US

A group of sick children took a boat ride with Prince William at Ullswater Lake, after he joined their steam boat in the Spring of 2009, for the return leg from Pooley Bridge to Glenridding Pier. William, who is patron of Mountain Rescue, was whisked to the steamer The Raven by Patterdale's rescue boat and climbed aboard for the final leg of its 18-mile round trip. One of the children, Harrison Holmes, who has mild cerebral palsy and chronic lung disease, was so enamoured with the prince that he held his hand for the whole journey and then invited him home for tea. William was meeting children, families and carers, chosen by the charity WellChild. Founded in 1977 to research kidney disease and originally named 'Kidney', it evolved over the years into the 'Children Nationwide Medical Research Foundation'

Top: a submarine under construction at BAE Systems. Above: The Raven.

before it broadened its remit to offer practical support for sick children and their families and was renamed WellChild in 2003.

MOUNT HELVELLYN

OS Grid NY 342151

Prince William braved torrential rain on a fell walk in 2009 to climb the third highest peak in England. He joined members of Cumbria's mountain rescue teams and children from the homeless charity Centrepoint to scale the 950-metre mountain in the Lakeland fells to raise a flag on Helvellyn to commemorate Cumbria's countdown to the London 2012 Olympics. The group was escorted up the mountain by members of Patterdale Mountain Rescue Team. 'The mountain rescue team guys do a fantastic job and they don't get the credit for doing the job they do,' William said. 'These men and women are unsung heroes. They are up and down these mountains rescuing people with broken legs every day.'

NEWBY BRIDGE

Great Tower Scout Activity Centre, Birks Road, Newby Bridge, Cumbria LA23 3PQ

Even though she is the Duchess of Cambridge, she still had to learn the ropes: so, in 2013, Kate braved the snowy weather to do an adventure training course with the Scout Association. She joined 24 other volunteers at the Great Tower Scout activity centre, close to the shore of Lake Windermere, in the heart of the Lake District. There she learnt how to supervise tree-climbing and rock-climbing and how to light a camp fire, removing her fingerless mittens to cook unleavened bread on a stick. 'It's actually not bad,' she joked, 'if you were really desperately hungry.' The Great Tower Scout Activity Centre, which is set in 250 acres, offers cubs and beaver scouts, a choice of both land and water-based adventures, including archery, low and high ropes, climbing and abseiling, sailing and canoeing. It has five lodges as well as camping sites. The Scout Association was founded in 1907 and has 32 million members worldwide (525,000 in the UK). Its 90,000 volunteers run 24,785 Beaver Scout Colonies, Cub Scout Packs, Scout Troops and Explorer Scout Units. Each year another 20,000 volunteers are trained but they are always in need of more as they have a 35,000-strong waiting list.

Top: Helvellyn, the third highest peak in England. Above: Kate at the Great Tower Scout Activity Centre.

GREATER MANCHESTER

MANCHESTER

Manchester Aquatics Centre, 2 Booth Street East, Manchester M13 9SS
The Willows Primary School, Tayfield Road Woodhouse Park, Manchester M22 1BQ

Both the Duke and Duchess of Cambridge have visited Manchester for official visits but for very different reasons: William was watching a water polo match while Kate was launching a new school counselling programme. The prince made his first visit to Manchester in 2009 to support the Great Britain team in the Women's World Water Polo Championship - it was the first water polo match he had seen since representing St Andrews University himself. William threw the ball into the centre of the 50-metre pool at Manchester Aquatics Centre, which was purpose built for the 2002 Commonwealth Games, to signal the start of the game (a group stage in the European Aquatics Championships) and watched Britain beat Slovakia. Afterwards he was presented with autographed balls by both sides. Four years later, the Duchess of Cambridge followed in his footsteps with a visit to the Willows Primary School, which is regarded as a beacon of hope on the tough Wythenshawe estate (inspiration for the gritty TV drama Shameless). Kate was launching a new counselling programme at the school, which has been rated as outstanding by Ofsted, for the children of drug and alcohol abusers. She was given a book entitled 'What Princesses Do' and read out a few extracts: '"Eat bananas" Yes. I certainly do that. "Dancing." Yes that too. "Eat sweets." Yes I like all those.' Kate was joined on the visit by comedian John Bishop, who was the ambassador for Comic Relief.

STOCKPORT

Vernon Park, Turncroft Lane, Stockport SK1 4AR

Above: The royal party visits a school sports day at Vernon Park, which had been granted Queen Elizabeth II Fields in Trust status.

During the Duke and Duchess of Cambridge's 2012 visit to the Midlands with the Queen, they paid a visit to Stockport's Vernon Park, which had been granted Queen Elizabeth II Fields in Trust status, for a school sports' day. William, who was patron of the Queen Elizabeth II Fields Challenge and is now President of the charity, and Kate competed to see how far they could throw a rocket-shaped foam javelin (William beat his wife by five feet). Kate also joined a group of Scouts, Cubs and Beavers playing games and racing to put up a tent. 'I do feel something of an interloper here today,' said William, paying tribute to his grandfather, who was at that time president of Fields in Trust. 'After all, the Queen has been patron of Fields In Trust for all 60 years of her reign. My grandfather, the Duke of Edinburgh, who very sadly cannot be here today, has been president for 64 years. This marvellous charity provides people of all ages up and down the country with the space to play sport, keep fit and generally get outside and enjoy themselves in the fresh air. Fields In Trust, I know, is very dear to my grandparents' hearts, as it is mine.' Founded in 1925, Fields in Trust set up the Queen Elizabeth II Fields Challenge to protect 2,012 outdoor recreational spaces as a permanent legacy to her Diamond Jubilee.

LANCASHIRE

BLACKBURN

St Aidan's Church of England Primary School, Norfolk Street, Mill Hill, Blackburn, Lancashire BB2 4EW

Witton Country Park, Preston Old Road, Blackburn, Lancashire BB2 2TP

As President of the Football Association, William is used to meeting premier league players. But when he visited Blackburn, in 2008, his footballing skills were put to the test. The prince was taking part in a kick about with pupils at St Aidan's Church of England primary school as part of the FA's Skills Programme, which aimed to give one million children in England coaching by 2010. Nathan Brown had the 'lifetime opportunity' of being coached by the prince, who practised dribbling with him. Three years later, the Duchess of Cambridge made her last official public appearance in Blackburn as a single girl. She and William visited Witton Country Park and were presented with a 'Courting Cake' – a heart-shaped shortbread cake, which was filled with raspberry jam and topped with their names on the icing. It is a Lancashire tradition, normally baked by the bride-to-be and given to her betrothed as a token of love, care and friendship. William, who was patron of the Queen Elizabeth II Fields Challenge (he is now President of Fields in Trust), took his fiancée to the 480-acre park, which has a visitors' centre with exhibitions of farm machinery, a natural history room and mammal centre, to sign a deed of dedication to protect its recreational space. Kate waved a flag to start a 100-metre race and placed a medal around the neck of winner Natalie Sailor.

Above right: William puts his footballing skills to the test.

DARWEN

Aldridge Community Academy, Sudell Road, Darwen, Lancashire BB3 3HD

Right: William and Kate wave as they leave Witton Country Park – Kate's last official public engagement as a single woman.

It was a rainy day in the market town of Darwen when the Duke and Duchess of Cambridge turned up three weeks before their wedding but they maintained their sunny countenances despite the weather. The couple had travelled north to open the Darwen Aldridge Community Academy, which aims to produce young enterpreneurs, and launch his new SkillForce Prince's Award. The Prince, who is patron of charity SkillForce, thanked his hosts for a 'warm if not a little damp' Lancastrian welcome, before saying: 'I know that I am very fortunate. I have the support of my family and friends, I do a job I enjoy ... and I have Catherine. But I have learnt through working with some truly inspiring charities – none more so than SkillForce – that these things can never be taken for granted.'

MERSEYSIDE

LIVERPOOL

Alder Hey Children's Hospital, Eaton Road, Liverpool L12 2AP
Brink Bar, 21 Parr Street, Liverpool L1 4JN

Both the Duke and Duchess of Cambridge have made official visits to Liverpool – and both have been to the Alder Hey Children's Hospital, one of only four stand-alone hospitals in the country caring for young people. William visited the hospital in 2010 to launch its Intra-Operative MRI scanner, the first of its kind in Europe and Kate followed suit on Valentine's Day two years later (when William was in the Falklands). On her first full 'away day', she was given a tour of the hospital - including the scanner, the oncology unit and the burns unit – and met some of the children being treated, who had made her (and William) Valentine's cards. When 12-year-old Megan Squire presented her with a card, with a picture of the couple on it, she said wistfully: 'Thank you so much. I'll make sure I show it to William when he gets back – which is not too far away now.' Kate also popped in to Ronald McDonald House, an independent charity, which provides accommodation for the families of sick children in hospitals across the country, and The Brink, a dry café bar. The Duchess, who is patron of the charity Action on Addiction, tried a smoothie named 'The Duchess' in her honour and was given a cupcake decorated with a heart – and she revealed, to the shame of men across the country, that William had managed to send her flowers and a card even though he was 7,900 miles away. The Brink, which is aimed at recovering alcoholics, donates its profits to Sharp, a treatment centre in the city run by Action on Addiction. The Alder Hey Children's NHS Foundation Trust provides care for over 275,000 children and young people every year – 60,000 children visit its A&E department each year while more than 30,000 attend as outpatients. Its Ronald McDonald House is the largest in the world with accommodation for 84 families a night.

Above: William unveils a child's painting on his visit to Alder Hey Children's Hospital. Right: Kate is given a warm welcome at Alder Hey when she makes a solo visit on Valentine's Day.

SCOTLAND

SCOTLAND

ALYTH

Jordanstone House, Blairgowrie, Nr Alyth, Perthshire PH11 8LY

The magnificent Georgian mansion Jordanstone House, on the outskirts of Alyth, was where the Middletons spent Christmas in 2006. They rented the £4,800-a-week property for the holiday season and invited Prince William to spend Hogmanay with them. But William failed to make an appearance, sparking rumours that his relationship with Kate was on the rocks. Months later the couple split – albeit temporarily. Set in rambling grounds, the 18th century mansion, which had belonged to the Conservative politician Sir James Duncan and his second wife Lady Beatrice (an actress known in her heyday for being the voice of Larry the Lamb in the Children's Hour series Toytown), was certainly fit for a prince. Crammed with antiques and old masters, the house still has its original two staircases (one for staff), a vast kitchen and laundry downstairs, a library of rare books and wood-panelled reception rooms with vast fireplaces upstairs, and 13 bedrooms furnished with four-poster beds.

Previous page: Balmoral Castle. Above: a fountain in the grounds of Jordanstone House. Right: the Georgian mansion, Jordanstone House, where the Middletons spent Christmas.

BALLATER

Balmoral Estates, Ballater, Aberdeenshire AB35 5TB

Bought for Queen Victoria in 1852 by Prince Albert, the Balmoral Estate, in the Scottish Highlands (the Queen owns Balmoral Castle while Prince Charles inherited Birkhall from his grandmother) is a favourite retreat of the royal family during the summer months. The Earl and Countess of Strathearn (as they are known north of the border) spent many weekends there when they were courting at St Andrews University. It was there that Kate was first spotted dressed in camouflage gear, lying in the heather, being coached by ghillies on how to

use a hunting rifle, causing outrage among animal rights protestors. It was also the place where the Middleton family was invited to a shooting party just before William and Kate announced their engagement. Set amongst the magnificent scenery of Royal Deeside, in the shadows of Lochnagar, the Balmoral Estate was described by Queen Victoria as her 'paradise in the Highlands'. Built by her husband in 1856 as a private home for her family, 100 yards from the original 15th century castle, Balmoral Castle has been handed down through successive generations of the royal family, who have made improvements (Prince Philip enlarged the flower and vegetable garden and created the water garden). Prince Charles inherited Birkhall on the death of the Queen Mother in 2002 – he spent his second honeymoon there in 2005. 'It is,' he said, 'such a special place, particularly because it was made by my grandmother. It is a childhood garden, and all I've done, really, is enhance it a bit.' He and the Duchess of Cornwall often undertake engagements locally (in 2006 Camilla launched the National Osteoporosis' Big Bone Walks while she was there). Built in 1715 and set in 53,000 acres on the River Muick, Prince Albert gifted Birkhall to his eldest son, Edward, Prince of Wales, when he bought the Balmoral Estate. But the future Edward VII only visited once (he preferred the larger Albergeldie Castle) so Queen Victoria bought Birkhall back for staff accommodation. During the 1930s, King George V lent Birkhall to the Duke and Duchess of York (later George VI and the Queen Mother), who holidayed there with the young Princesses Elizabeth and Margaret. The Yorks were extremely fond of the house, which they redecorated, replanting the garden, but moved to Balmoral when George VI ascended the throne in 1936. After her husband's death and her daughter's accession to the throne, the Queen Mother moved back to Birkhall, using the house as a summer residence. Birkhall is not open to the public but the Balmoral estate grounds, gardens and castle ballroom are opened to visitors between April and July.

Above: The Queen's Scottish residence Balmoral Castle, which has been owned by the royal family since the Victorian era.

BRAEMAR

Princess Royal and Duke of Fife Memorial Park, Braemar, Aberdeenshire AB35 5YX

Above: three generations of royals at the annual Braemar Gathering.

The annual Braemar Gathering is a favourite of the royal family, who are regular visitors. In 2005, Prince William joined his grandparents at the procession, chatting to them in the royal box as they watched a tug-of-war competition, Highland dancing and a veterans' parade and listened to the pipes and drums of the 1st Battalion The Highlanders and the Gordon Highlanders Regimental Association. While there have been Gatherings at Braemar since the days of King Malcolm Canmore, a century ago, the current gathering is run by the Braemar Royal Highland Charity, of which the Queen is Patron – it maintains the 12-acre Princess Royal and Duke of Fife Memorial Park with the proceeds. Large crowds turn up each year to acclaim their Monarch as Chieftain of the Braemar Gathering. Its foot races are some of the oldest in the world.

COLDSTREAM

The Hirsel Country Park, Coldstream, Berwickshire TD12 4LW

This 3,000-acre estate, which has been the seat of her family since the 17th century was the reception venue for the 2008 wedding of teacher Lady Iona Douglas-Home and her banker husband Thomas Hewitt, son of the 9th Viscount Lifford. The granddaughter of the late Prime Minister, Sir Alec Douglas-Home, and daughter of Coutts chairman David, 15th Earl of Home, has known the The Earl and Countess of Strathearn since they were all at university in Scotland. The Hirsel dates back to the 17th century when the first Earl of Home contracted to buy the estate but it was not until 1621 that James VI finally granted the lands of Hirsel to James, the 2nd Earl of Home. It is renowned for its salmon fishing on the river Tweed (in 1743 the 8th Earl caught a 69lb salmon on a 22' rod and a horse hair line). The estate was merged with the Douglas Estate in Lanarkshire after the marriage of the 11th Earl of Home, who was Under Secretary of State for Foreign Affairs and Keeper of the Great Seal of Scotland, and Lady Lucy Elizabeth Montagu-Scott. Its most famous inhabitant was Sir Alec Douglas-Home, the 14th Earl of Home, who served in the House of Lords before renouncing his title in 1963 to become Prime Minister.

CRATHIE

Crathie Kirk, Crathie, Aberdeenshire AB35 5UL

Set in the tiny village of Crathie, at the entrance to Balmoral Castle, this parish church has been attended by the royal family since the reign of Queen Victoria, who laid the foundation stone. She caused a scandal by worshipping in Scotland until she pointed out that she was Queen of Scotland as well as head of the Church of England. The royals worship at Crathie Kirk when they are at Balmoral – the south transept (with its porched entrance) is reserved for them and the central panel in the carved pew has the Royal and Imperial monogram of Queen Victoria. Princess Anne married her second husband, Royal Navy Commander, Timothy Laurence, at the Kirk, and the royal family attended the Sunday service there on August 31, 1997, after the death of Princess Diana. Built in the 19th century, overlooking the ruins of the original 14th century church, the interior of the church is richly-decorated and shows a long association with the royal family. Its large stained glass window in the south gable was gifted by Queen Victoria and the church has large marble busts in each corner of Queen Victoria, George V and George VI, as well as a memorial to the Queen Mother. The church graveyard contains the headstone of Queen Victoria's personal servant John Brown, whose friendship with the Queen was documented in the film Mrs Brown.

Top: The Hirsel Country Park. Left: Crathie Kirk, where the royals worship when at Balmoral.

CRIEFF

Glenturret Distillery, The Hosh, Crieff, Perthshire PH7 4HA
MacRosty Park, Milnab Street, Crieff, Perthshire PH7 4BH
Strathearn Community Campus, Pittenzie Road, Crieff, Perthshire PH7 3JN

The Earl and Countess of Strathearn made their first joint appearance in the market town of Crieff after returning from their 2014 tour of Australia. The couple visited Strathearn Community Campus, where they were welcomed by pipes and drums, met local Scouts, Cadets and Brownies and were given a tour of a Scottish Ambulance helicopter (call sign Helimed 76) – shortly before William announced he was joining the East Anglia Air Ambulance service. William and Kate, who was wearing a delicate silver broach in the shape of a Celtic knot, were then whisked off to MacRosty park, where they unveiled a plaque commemorating the park's designation as a Queen Elizabeth II Fields in Trust (William took over as President of Fields in Trust in 2013), and were given a teddy bear (wearing a Strathearn tartan kilt) for Prince George. The park, which has an old water mill, bandstand and café (housed in the old tennis pavilion) had just been restored. The couple then toured the Glenturret distillery, where Famous Grouse is made. After being encouraged to pour themselves a shot of whisky from a barrel, William threw caution to the wind and downed a glass of 68.9 per cent, straight from the still. 'I'll give anything a go. I will probably regret it later,' he laughed before squeaking: 'That's pretty busy.' He then offered a glass to his wife, who normally shies away from drinking in public. Declining his offer, she plumped for a dram of The Naked Grouse. 'I'll stick with that girlie one,' she laughed. Scotland's favourite whisky was created in 1897 by Matthew Gloag, whose grandfather founded the family wine and spirit business. His daughter Philippa designed its distinctive red grouse label and his signature is on every bottle.

Above: William and Kate are shown round Glenturret Distillery by Famous Grouse Experience manager Stuart Cassells. Left: whisky tasting.

CUMNOCK

Dumfries House, Cumnock, Ayrshire KA18 2NJ

Above: the Palladian mansion, Dumfries House, which Prince Charles saved for the nation.

When the Countess of Strathearn joined her husband and father-in-law on a 2013 visit to the 18th century stately home Dumfries House she did not expect to come face to face with her double. But, as the trio opened its new Tamar Manoukian Outdoor Centre, she was given a replica doll. 'Oh no. Is that me?' she asked. 'Is that meant to be me? Does my hair really look like that?' Schoolgirl Danya Miller, who owned the £15 doll, said: 'I told her she was much prettier than the doll and her hair was not nearly so big and she laughed and seemed happy.' William and Kate joined Prince Charles at the Palladian mansion, which he saved for the nation after forming a consortium to buy it for £45 million (he was accused of a 'reckless gamble' after using £20 million from the Prince's Trust). They were greeted by children from the uniformed youth services Youth United, who competed in an obstacle race, before watching a fly past by three Typhoons from 6 squadron RAF Leuchars. William, too, showed he had a sense of humour. When handed a Lee's Macaroon bar, he joked: 'Oh, the missus is coming – I'll have to give it to her.' Dumfries House, which combines the neo-classical architecture of Robert Adam with the furniture of Thomas Chippendale, was owned by the Marquess of Bute, former racing driver Johnny Dumfries.

EDINBURGH

Canongate Kirk, 153 Canongate, Edinburgh EH8 8BN
Palace of Holyroodhouse, Canongate, Edinburgh EH8 8DX
St Giles' Cathedral, High Street, Edinburgh EH1 1RE

Above: the Queen's official Scottish residence, the Palace of Holyroodhouse.

The Earl and Countess of Strathearn have made two visits to the Scottish capital since their marriage. The first was in 2011 when they flew up to Scotland on the budget airline FlyBe for the wedding of William's cousin Zara Phillips and former England Rugby captain Mike Tindall – the first royal wedding in Scotland in 20 years and the largest gathering of royals (including the Queen and Prince Philip) since their own wedding. William, Kate – and Prince Harry - joined the couple on the eve of the wedding for a cocktail party on board the decommissioned Royal yacht Britannia. They spent the night at the Queen's official Scottish residence (where Zara spent her final night as a single woman) before walking to the 17th century church, the official Kirk of the Palace of Holyroodhouse, on the city's ancient Royal Mile. Zara (reportedly the Queen's favourite granddaughter) was accompanied to the church by her father Captain Mark Phillips, driving the several yards down the Royal Mile in a Bentley. The Monarch and Prince Philip, who were the last guests to arrive at the church, sat in the royal pew, which bears the coat of arms of the Queen, the Duke of Edinburgh and

Duke of Rothesay, surmounted by an exact replica of the Hours of Scotland (the crown, sceptre and sword). After the ceremony, in which a choir of 15 boys and girls from Zara's old Scottish boarding school Gordonstoun performed, the couple returned by Bentley to the Palace of Holyroodhouse, which was founded as a monastery in 1128, and was once home to Mary Queen of Scots (George VI ordered that her apartments were preserved sacred from every alteration).

Our current Queen spends a week at the Palace of Holyroodhouse every summer carrying out official engagements – audiences, investitures and the royal garden party, a tradition started by her grandparents King George V and Queen Mary. At the start of her visit, she is presented with the Keys of the City of Edinburgh on a red velvet cushion. (The Scottish variant of the Royal Standard is flown when she is in residence and the Royal Company of Archers form her ceremonial bodyguard.) The second visit the Earl and Countess paid to Scotland was a year later when William was made a Knight of the Thistle by his grandmother to mark her Diamond Jubilee and his 30th birthday. Wearing a moss green velvet gown and distinctive heron-plumed hat, he was inducted into the Order of the Thistle, in its dedicated chapel in St Giles' Cathedral. The Order, which was set up by James II (James VII of Scotland) is unique to Scotland and is in the personal gift of the Queen. St Giles' Cathedral, with its famed crown spire, stands on the Royal Mile (at the other end from Canongate Kirk) between the Palace of Holyroodhouse and Edinburgh Castle. The current Gothic cathedral, which is dedicated to the patron saint of Edinburgh, dates from the 14th century but was greatly renovated in the 19th century. Every year the Queen donates a Christmas tree from Balmoral.

Above left: Kate and William attend the wedding of William's cousin Zara Philipps and rugby player Mike Tindall.
Left: St Giles' cathedral with its famous crowned spire.

FASLANE

HM Naval Base Clyde, Faslane, Helensburgh, Dunbartonshire G84 8HL

Prince William went on a morale-boosting trip to the Bay of Faslane in 2010 – a week after HMS Astute ran aground off the Isle of Skye. The Prince, who is Commodore-in-Chief, Submarines, attended a dedication service at HM Naval Base Clyde (commonly known as Faslane) and named the base as the 'Home of Submariners'. William, who trained on the vessels in 2008, as part of a two-month attachment to the Royal Navy, then joked and laughed with submariners as he presented them with 'Gold Deterrent Pins' for long service. Built during World War II, HM Naval Base Clyde is the Royal Navy's headquarters in Scotland (and one of three operating bases in the UK) and is best known as the home of Britain's nuclear submarines armed with Trident missiles.

FORTEVIOT

Forteviot Village Hall, Forteviot, Perthshire PH2 9BT
St Andrew's Church, Forteviot, Perthshire PH2 9BT

It was an alcoholic day for the Earl and Countess of Strathearn when they visited a fete in the village of Forteviot on the bank of the River Earn. The couple had already been sampling whisky at the Famous Grouse Experience, when they were offered a sip of gin from Strathearn Distillery. 'I had better not drink too much,' Kate said, 'because of all the whisky I drank at Glenturret.' The couple was shown around the village fete, which was specially convened in their honour, on May Day 2014, by John Dewar, the current Lord Forteviot, a scion of the Dewar whisky dynasty. His grandfather John Alexander Dewar, 1st Lord Forteviot, rebuilt the village in the 1920s. After a tour of the stalls in the square, and a display of Scottish dancing, Kate went to look at the art on display in the village hall while William visited the church. Ever the horseman, he stopped to inspect some of the horses ridden by the local pony club and was rewarded with a lick from a cheeky palomino. The village of Fonteviot was put on the map in 2009 when archaeologists discovered an early Bronze Age tomb – they found burial treasures, including a bronze and gold dagger, a wooden bowl and leather bag, alongside the ancient ruler.

Above: HMS Astute.

GLASGOW

BAE Systems, 1471 South St, Scotstoun, Glasgow G14 0XN
Donald Dewar Leisure Centre, 220 Garscadden Road, Drumchapel, Glasgow G15 8SX
Emirates Arena and Sir Chris Hoy Velodrome, 1000 London Road, Glasgow G40 3HG
Quarriers Project, Unit 25, KCEDG Commercial Centre, Ladyloan Place, Drumchapel,
Glasgow G158LB

When he was an officer in the Blues and Royals – part of the Household Cavalry – Prince William made his first visit to Glasgow and was given a guided tour of the world's most advanced warship HMS Daring. The ship, which was launched by the Countess of Wessex, was the first of a batch of six Type 45 destroyers ordered by the Royal Navy from BAE Systems. William visited the shipyard, where the 7,000-ton £1 billion vessel was built, in 2007, in the run-up to his two-month attachment with the Royal Navy. He toured the armoured operations room and visited the bridge where he tried out the captain's chair. 'It's a bit like a dentist's chair,' he joked, pointing to an array of switches and controls. Six years later, in the run-up to the Commonwealth Games, he returned to the city on a two-day visit with his wife, to open its £113 million Emirates Arena. On the way into the arena, William spotted four-year-old Shona Ritchie in the crowd, dressed as a princess with a crown and holding a flower. 'Ooh. Is that for me?' said William before she thrust it in Kate's direction. 'No. You want to give it to Kate. Quite right.' Shona had been waiting all day to catch a glimpse of the prince but - after plucking up the courage to ask him for a kiss - she pulled away and left him kissing the air. Inside the arena, the Duke and Duchess, who was six months pregnant, watched aspiring athletes from the Glasgow School of Sport train in athletics, track cycling, badminton, football and netball. They visited the Sir Chris Hoy Velodrome (named after the most-decorated Olympic cyclist of all time) and chatted with Games mascot Clyde and its creator, Beth Gilmour (the thistle mascot asked if he could pat Kate's bump). Afterwards the couple launched a Scottish pilot of their Coach Core initiative at the Glasgow Club Donald Dewar – the charity was launched by the Royal Foundation before the 2012 Olympic Games to inspire the next generation to become sports coaches. During his speech, Prince William said his wife 'had to hold herself back' from 'grabbing a racquet' and joining in with the tennis. 'She is limited a little in the sports she can play right now,' he added. Instead the couple played a game of table tennis before Kate tried her hand at basketball (she scored on her ninth shot). Finally they paid a visit to the Quarriers Stopover Project, a homeless charity, which provides short-term accommodation for young people, and training facilities. William donned headphones to play DJ while Kate turned producer, calling 'cut' on a filming session. Two years later the couple were back in Glasgow with Prince Harry, watching the Commonwealth Games. Kate also attended a reception for the charity Sports Aid, of which she is patron, and met former world and Commonwealth swimming champion James Hickman. She told him that Prince George 'loves the water and grabs things to splash with'. William attended a thanksgiving event for the organisers of the games.

Top: William and Kate at the £113 million Emirates Arena. Middle: The couple at Glasgow's Donald Dewar Leisure Centre. Bottom: William takes to the hockey pitch.

HAWICK

Johnstons of Elgin, East Field Mills, Mansfield Road, Hawick, Roxburghshire TD9 8AA

Royal warrant holder Johnstons of Elgin is believed to have created the cashmere jumper Prince George wore on his first Mothering Sunday. Prince Charles, who is chairman of the 'Campaign for Wool' visited the company's mill in Hawick with the Duchess of Cornwall a month before his birth and awarded them a royal warrant. The family-run firm Johnstons of Elgin, which was founded in 1797, has the last remaining vertical mill in Scotland: the mill in Elgin is where all its tweed is woven. It has another knitting mill in Hawick, which is where Prince George's jumper is believed to have been made. Visitors can tour both mills and see the manufacturing process from start to finish.

KELSO

St Andrew's Episcopal Church, Belmont Place, Kelso, Roxburghshire TD5 7JB

Prince William was so desperate to get to the 2008 wedding of Iona Douglas-Home, a teacher, and banker Thomas Hewitt that he bent the rules and flew 260 miles in a Chinook helicopter at a cost to the country of £18,522. (The MoD claimed it was 'a legitimate training sortie'.) He joined Kate and Harry at St Andrew's Church, which has original stencils on the chancel ceiling, before going to the reception in Coldstream. The present building, which lies opposite the ruins of Kelso Abbey, was designed in 1869 by leading Scottish architect Sir Robert Anderson, who also designed the altar, reredos and font. The wooden panelling of its inner porch was a gift from Lord Home, after the demolition of the chapel at Hirsel.

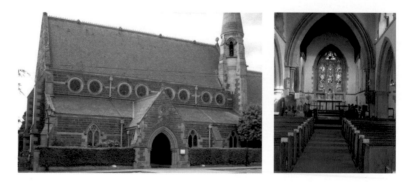

Above and right: the 19th century St Andrew's Church in Kelso.

ST ANDREWS

Balgove Farmhouse, Strathtyrum Farm, St Andrews, Fife KY16 9SF
Kinkell Farm, Kinkell, St Andrews, Fife KY16 8PN
Ma Bells, St Andrews Hotel du Vin, 40 The Scores, St Andrews, Fife KY16 9AS
University of St Andrews, 8 The Scores, St Andrews, Fife KY16 9AZ
Upper Flat, 13a Hope Street, St Andrews, Fife KY16 9HJ
West Port Bar, 170 South Street, St Andrews, Fife KY16 9EG

Above: William and Kate return to St Andrews University for its 600th anniversary appeal.

Set in the tiny seaside town of St Andrews on the east coast of Scotland (once the ecclesiastical capital of Scotland and now renowned as the home of golf) the University of St Andrews was founded in 1413 and is the oldest university in Scotland. Boasting alumni such as King James II of Scotland, Nobel Prize winner Sir James Black, Edward Jenner, who discovered the smallpox vaccine, First Minister of Scotland Alex Salmond and novelist Fay Weldon, its most famous old students are the Earl and Countess of Strathearn. They first met in 2001 (Kate arrived for freshers' week; William a week later) when they moved into the same halls of residence St Salvator's Hall (deemed the best because it is set on the quadrangle) and began studying for the same degree (history of art – although William later changed to geography). But it was not until their second term when Kate caught the eye of the prince by sashaying down the catwalk in her lingerie during a charity fashion show. By their second year the couple were close enough to share a £400,000 maisonette in the centre of the town, which they rented for £400-a-week with two friends Fergus Boyd and Olivia Bleasdale. The students kept a low profile, walking or cycling to lectures, shopping at Safeway and spending the evenings at home, listening to the sound of William's R&B music or Fergus' jazz, thumping from their stereos. They rarely ventured out during the week - unless they were attending lectures or visiting the university library - apart from on Wednesday afternoons when they played sport. Both William, who had by now been voted the university's water polo captain, and Fergus trained for two hours on Thursday nights in the pool of St Leonards girls' school. For their final two years, the group moved away from the centre of the town into a £750,000 18th century farmhouse on the Strathyrum estate. The cottage, set in rolling grounds brimming with orchids and fuschia bushes, was an idyllic venue for William and Kate. Not only was the house discreet, but it was also totally secure: a neighbouring cottage was chosen as the centre of a security operation, and squads of officers were drafted in to keep 24-hour surveillance on the farmhouse. The cottage was also bombproofed and CCTV cameras and panic buttons installed, linked to both local police stations and Buckingham Palace in case of an emergency. During their time at the university, the couple immersed themselves in student life. They were often to be spotted drinking and chatting at Ma Bells, the bar in the basement of the St Andrews Golf Hotel (now the Hotel du Vin), which is close to the university and overlooks the seafront. Known as 'yah yah Bells' because of its reputation as a hangout for the university's Sloane Rangers, it was often heaving in the evenings with students dancing to the resident DJ. Another favourite venue was the West Port Bar, where William and Fergus retired after playing rugby sevens. One of

their annual outings was the May Ball, which was held in the Byre, a converted barn, in the grounds of Kinkell Farm – the royal couple had VIP passes so they could avoid the riff-raff. When the couple graduated in 2005, the university's vice chancellor Dr Brian Lang, said: 'I say this every year to all new graduates: "You may have met your husband or wife." Our title as the top matchmaking university in Britain signifies so much that is good about St Andrews, so we rely on you to go forth and multiply – but in the positive sense that I earlier urged you to adopt.' Six years later, William and Kate returned to the university for its 600th Anniversary Appeal, of which William was patron. By then they were engaged.

Top: St Andrews University. Above left: the Hope Street maisonette, which Kate shared with William. Above middle: the Hotel du Vin. Above right: Balgove Farmhouse where William and Kate spent their final two years at university.

PHOTO CREDITS

Jacket front and back: @OIC Photos; pages 2 and 3: Llandwyn Beach @Terry Winter; page 8: Introduction: Kate's Christening @OIC Photos; Jimmy's Cambridge @Jimmy's Cambridge; Goole Academy @Goole Academy. SOUTH WEST: Page 9: cover: St Nicholas' Church @Rex Harris; page 10: Cornwall: Falmouth: The Chain Locker and Shipwrights Pub @Roger Marks; Padstow: The National Lobster Hatchery in Cornwall @Coastal Company; page 11: Devon: Dartmouth: Britannia Royal Naval College @PA; Tiverton: St Peter's Church @Roy Webber; page 12 Dorset: Bovington: Bovington Garrison @PA; Portland: Weymouth and Portland National Sailing Academy @Royal Yachting Association; page 13 Gloucestershire: Cheltenham: Cheltenham Racecourse @The Jockey Club; page 14: Cherington: St Nicholas' Church @ Rex Harris; page 15: Cirencester: Cirencester Park Polo Club @OIC Photos; page 16: Coates: The Tunnel House Inn @The Tunnel House Inn; pages 17 and 18: Doughton: Highgrove House @Gap Photos; page 19: Eastleach: Macaroni Wood @OIC Photos; page 20: Minchinhampton: Gatcombe Park @Kit Houghton; Northleach: St Peter and St Paul's Church @St Peter and St Paul's Church; page 21: Westonbirt: Beaufort Polo Club @OIC Photos; page 22: Somerset: Bishops Lydeard: St Mary's Church @Michael Hansford; page 23: Wiltshire: East Knoyle: Clouds House @Louis Austin; page 24: Lacock: St Cyriac's Church @St Cyriac's Church; page 25: Malmesbury: Malmesbury Abbey @Rex Harris; page 26: Marlborough: Marlborough College @Allan Harris; page 27: Tidworth: Tedworth House @Help for Heroes; page 28: Wilton: St Mary and St Nicholas's Church @Rex Harris. SOUTH EAST: Page 29: cover: Osborne House @John Martin; page 30: Berkshire: Ascot: Ascot Racecourse @Peter Shakesneff; page 31: Coworth Park @Dorchester Collection @OIC Photos; page 32: Ashampstead Common: Party Pieces @Imogen Ware; Bradfield: St Andrew's Church @Rex Harris; page 33: Bradfield Southend: Kate as Brownie @OIC Photos; Kate as schoolgirl @OIC Photos; Bradfield Church of England Primary School @Imogen Ware; West View @Imogen Ware; page 34: Bucklebury: Michael and Carole Middleton @PA; The Bladebone Inn @Imogen Ware; St Mary's Church @Rosa Foulger; Peach's Stores @Imogen Ware; page 35: Burnham: Dorothy and Ronald Goldsmith @OIC Photos; Cold Ash: Downe House @Imogen Ware; page 36: Dorney: St James The Less Church @Alan Gillespie; page 37: Englefield: St Mark's Church @Rex Harris; page 38: Eton: Eton College @Dhaneesha Senaratne; Prince William @OIC Photos; page 39: Lambourn: St Michael and All Angels @Andrew Snowdon; page 40: Pangbourne: St Andrew's School @St Andrew's School; page 41: Reading: Carole and Kate @OIC Photos; Slough: 33 Arborfield Close @Imogen Ware; Stanford Dingley: The Old Boot Inn @Imogen Ware; pages 42, 43 and 44: Windsor: Victoria Barracks @OIC Photos; Windsor Castle @Ramon Ruti; St George's Chapel @The Dean and Canons of Windsor; page 45: Wokingham: Ludgrove School @PA; Yattendon: The Estate Office @Imogen Ware; page 46: Buckinghamshire: Milton Keynes: Bletchley Park @OIC Photos; page 47: Saunderton: Child Bereavement UK @Derek Pelling, @Ian Jones; page 48: Hampshire: Aldershot: Mons Barracks @OIC Photos; page 49: Gosport: The Royal Navy Submarine Museum @Royal Navy Submarine Museum; page 50: Hook: RAF Odiham @Crown Copyright 2015; page 51: Southampton: Ocean Terminal @Princess Cruises; page 52: Sutton Scotney: Naomi House @Naomi House; page 53: Isle of Wight: Cowes: The Anchor Inn @JJ Myers; page 54: East Cowes: Osborne House @John Martin; page 55: Kent: Wrotham: Margaret McMillan House @Wide Horizons; page 56: Oxfordshire: Bledington: The King's Head Inn @The King's Head Inn; page 57: Burford: St John the Baptist's Church @John Ward; page 58: Carterton: RAF Brize Norton @PA; Ewelme: St Mary the Virgin's Church @Brian Smales; Nettlebed: St Bartholomew's Church @ John Ward; page 59: Oxford: Oxford Spires Academy and Rose Hill Primary School @The Art Room; page 60: Rotherfield Greys: St Nicholas' Anglican Church @Rex Harris; page 61: Witney: Cogges Manor Farm Museum @Cogges Manor Farm Museum; page 62: Surrey: East Molesey: Royal School of Needlework @Royal School of Needlework; Epsom: Epsom Downs Racecourse @Michael Church; page 63: Sandhurst: Royal Military Academy @PA; page 64: Sutton: Royal Marsden @Debbie Binner. LONDON & GREATER LONDON: Page 65: cover: Palace of Westminster @Chris Fulcher; page 66: Art & Culture: BAFTA @OIC Photos; BFI Southbank @Chris Jackson/Getty; page 67: London Palladium @OIC Photos; page 68: The O2 @O2; Odeon: @OIC Photos; page 69: Royal Albert Hall @OIC Photos; page 70: Royal Opera House @Allan Harris, @Henry Peterman; page 72: Banks & Brokers (& the law): HSBC @Centrepoint; page 73: Bars & Clubs: Boujis @Boujis; Loulou's @author; Mahiki @Mahiki; page 74: Raffles @Raffles; Roof Gardens @Roof Gardens; Tonteria @author; Whisky Mist @Whisky Mist; page 75: Britain's Heritage: Australia House @The Flinders Committee; Banqueting House @G Macdonald; page 76: Cenotaph @OIC Photos; Goldsmiths' Hall @OIC Photos; Guildhall @Guildhall; page 77: Horse Guards Parade @OIC Photos; Middle Temple Inn @Middle Temple Inn; pages 79 and 80: Tower of London @Nicola Jones, @OIC Photos; page 81: Churches & Cathedrals: Guards' Chapel @Crown Copyright 2015; Holy Trinity Church @OIC Photos; page 81: St Luke's Church @Andy Ware; page 82: St Paul's Cathedral @Steve McClean; pages 83 and 84: Westminster Abbey @Angie Middleton, @OIC Photos; page 85: Hospitals: Great Ormond Street Hospital @Great Ormond Street Hospital; page 86: King Edward VII Hospital @OIC Photos; The Royal Marsden @The Royal Marsden; page 87: St Mary's Hospital @OIC Photos; pages 88 and 89: Hotels: Claridge's @Tusk/Chris Jackson/Getty, @OIC Photos; page 90: The Dorchester @The Dorchester Collection; The Goring @The Goring; page 91: Grosvenor House @Marriott Hotels; Royal Garden Hotel @Royal Garden Hotel; page 92: Lancaster Hotel @Lancaster Hotel; The Savoy @Fairmont Hotels; page 93: Museums & Galleries: Dulwich Picture Gallery @Dulwich Picture Gallery; page 94: Imperial War Museum @OIC Photos; Madame Tussauds @Madame Tussauds; page 95: National Maritime Museum @Lloyd Images/Ben Ainslee; page 96: National Portrait Gallery @OIC Photos; Natural History Museum @ Adam Raoof; page 97: Royal Academy of Arts @Fraser Marr; The Royal Society @Tusk/Chris Jackson/Getty; page 98: Saatchi Gallery @Andy Ware; Sladmore Contemporary Art Gallery @Child Bereavement UK; page 99: V&A Museum of Childhood @V&A; London Zoo @ZSL; page 100: Patronages: Centrepoint @Centrepoint; Hope House @OIC Photos; page 101: Only Connect @OIC; Shooting Star House Children's Hospice @Andy Newbold; page 102: Pubs & Restaurants: L'Anima @L'Anima; The Bluebird @The Bluebird; Builders Arms @Andy Ware; page 103: Bumpkin @Ignite Group; The Collection @author; Dans Le Noir @Dans Le Noir; page 104: The Hambrough Tavern @OIC Photos; The Troubadour Café @The Troubadour Café; pages 105 and 106: Royal Residences:

Buckingham Palace @Angie Middleton; the kiss @OIC Photos; page 107 Clarence House @James Clark; the engagement @OIC Photos; page 108: 57 Clarence Street @OIC Photos; Kensington Palace @Harriet Armstrong; pages 109 and 110: 20 Kingsbridge Road @OIC Photos; Old Church Street @Andy Ware; St James' Palace @Andy Ware, @Herry Lawford; page 111: Schools: Bacon's College @author; Blessed Sacrament Roman Catholic Primary School @Place2Be; Leiths School of Food and Wine @Leiths; page 112: Minors Nursery School @PA; Northolt High School @The Art Room; page 113: Old Ford Primary School @Martyn Milner/The Scout Association; Robert Blair Primary School @author; Wetherby Pre-Prep School @PA; page 114: Shops: Alexander McQueen @Andy Ware; Alice Temperley @Andy Ware; Asprey @Asprey; page 115: Blue Almonds @Blue Almonds; Boomf @Boomf; Burlington Arcade @Burlington Arcade; Cath Kidston @Debbie Wallwork; page 116: Fortnum & Mason @Fortnum & Mason; page 117: Garrard @Garrard; Gieves & Hawkes @Gieves & Hawkes; Jigsaw @Jigsaw; page 118: John Lobb Bootmaker @John Lobb; Patrick Mavros @Patrick Mavros; Peter Jones @Andy Ware; page 119: Rachel Riley @Rachel Riley; page 120: Richard Ward Salon @Andy Ware; Shane Connolly @author; Smythson @Charlotte Burges; page 121: The Shop at Bluebird @The Shop at Bluebird; Trotters @Trotters; Turnbull & Asser @Turnbull @Asser; page 122: Sport: The All England Lawn Tennis and Croquet Club @OIC Photos; pages 123 and 124: Brentford: GSK Human Performance Lab @author; Queen Elizabeth Olympic Park @Queen Elizabeth Olympic Park; @OIC Photos; page 125 Twickenham Stadium @RFU; Wembley Stadium @FA; Westway Sports Centre @Westway Sports Centre; page 126: Transport: Baker Street tube @OIC Photos; Routemaster Bus @Shutterstock. EAST OF ENGLAND: page 127: cover St John's College @ Judy Dean; pages 128, 129 and 130: Cambridgeshire: Cambridge: Guildhall @Cambridge City Council; Jimmy's Cambridge @Jimmy's Cambridge; St John's College @Judy Dean; page 131: Essex: Chelmsford: Hylands Park @Richard Wilkins; page 132: Hertfordshire: Leavesden: Warner Bros Studios @Martin Cummings; pages 133 and 134: Norfolk: Anmer: Anmer Hall @Janna; Castle Rising: Castle Rising @OIC Photos; page 135: East Raynham: St Mary's Church @Janna; Fakenham: Thursford Collection @OIC Photos; page 136: Gayton: St Nicholas' Church @Stan Watkinson; Gayton Hall @OIC Photos; page 137: Great Massingham: The Dabbling Duck @Jeff Jessop; Norwich: Norfolk Showground @EACH; pages 138 and 139: Sandringham: The Sandringham Estate @Joan Berry; page 140 Snettisham: St Mary's Church @Gary Brothwell; Tattersett @Janna; page 141: Suffolk: Fressingfield: Fox and Goose @Fox and Goose; page 142: Ipswich: The Treehouse Centre @EACH; page 143: Westleton: The Westleton Crown @Agellus Hotels; page 144: Wingfield: De La Pole Arms @Jean McCreanor; St Andrew's Church @St Andrew's Church. EAST MIDLANDS: cover page 145 and page 146: Derbyshire: Bakewell: Chatsworth House @Jacqueline Poggi; page 147: Leicestershire: Fleckney: Fiona Cairns @Fiona Cairns; Leicester: De Montfort University @Jack O'Sullivan; page 148: Lincolnshire: Grimsby: National Fishing Heritage Centre @OIC Photos; Sleaford: RAF Cranwell @PA; page 149: Stoke Rochford: St Andrew and St Mary's Church @Eric Lomax; page 150: Nottinghamshire: Nottingham: Council House @Nottingham City Council. WEST MIDLANDS: page 151: cover: Coventry Cathedral @Ed Webster; page 152: Birmingham: Library of Birmingham @Library of Birmingham; South & City College @South & City College; page 153: Coventry: War Memorial Park @Mark Radford; page 154: Shropshire: Shrewsbury: RAF Shawbury @PA; page 155: Staffordshire: Alrewas: National Memorial Arboretum @Susan Lawrance; Burton on Trent: St. George's Park @Chris Jackson/The FA/Getty; page 156: Rocester: JCB World Headquarters @Derby Telegraph. WALES: Page 157: cover: Llandwynn Beach @ Terry Winter; page 158: Bodorgan: Bodorgan Estates @ Steve Ashton; page 159: Cardiff: Llandaff Cathedral @Michael Curi; page 160: Holyhead: RAF Valley @PA; The Showground @OIC Photos; page 161: Llanddwyn Beach: Llanddwyn Beach @Terry Winter; Llandudno: St Dunstan's Centre @Blind Veterans; page 162: Llantrisant: Royal Mint @Royal Mint; Merthyr Tydfil: Central Beacons Mountain Rescue @Central Beacons Mountain Rescue Team; page 163: Pembroke: The Valero Pembroke Refinery @Valero; Rhoscolyn: White Eagle Pub @White Eagle Pub; page 164: Trearddur Bay: Lifeboat Station @OIC Photos. YORKSHIRE & THE HUMBER: Page 165: cover: Harewood House @Harewood House Trust; page 166: East Riding of Yorkshire: Goole: Goole Academy @Goole Academy; page 167: Kingston Upon Hull: Associated British Ports @Crown Copyright 2015; page 168: North Yorkshire: Aldborough: St Andrew's Church @St Andrew's Church; Allerton Mauleverer: Allerton Castle @Chris Chambers; page 169: Harrogate: West Park @OIC Photos; York: RAF Linton-on-Ouse @PA; page 170: South Yorkshire: Rotherham: Healthbeds @Healthbeds; pages 171 and 172: West Yorkshire: Leeds: Harewood House @Harewood House Trust, @Memooma Butt. NORTH EAST: Page 173: cover: Alnwick Castle @David Ford; page 174: Northumberland: Alnwick: St Michael's Church @St Michael's Church/Reverend Denis Sweetman; page 175: Teeside: Stockton-on-Tees: CRI Stockton @PA; page 176: Tyne and Wear: Gateshead: Gateshead Youth Council @The Key; page 177: Hetton-Le-Hole @OIC Photos; pages 178 and 179: Newcastle upon Tyne: Elswick Park @Steve Brock/Fields in Trust; page 180: South Shields: Haven Point Leisure Centre @South Tyneside Council. NORTH WEST: Page 181: cover: The Lake District @Matthew Breach; page 182: Cheshire: Chester: Chester Cathedral @Chester Cathedral; page 183: Cumbria: Barrow-in-Furness: BAE Systems @Crown Copyright 2015; Glenridding: The Raven @Richard Ratcliffe; page 184: Mount Helvellyn @Mark Vanstone; Newby Bridge: Great Tower Scout Activity Centre @Martyn Milner/The Scout Association; page 185: Greater Manchester: Stockport: Vernon Park @Fields In Trust; page 186 and 187: Blackburn: St Aidan's Church of England primary school @Lancashire Evening Post; Witton Country Park @Fields in Trust; page 188: Merseyside: Liverpool: Alder Hey Children's Hospital @Alder Hey NHS Trust. SCOTLAND: Page 189: cover: Balmoral @Neil Rogers; page 190: Alyth: Jordanstone House @Scotts Castle Holidays; page 191: Ballater: Balmoral Estates @Neil Roger; page 192: Braemar @PA; page 193: Coldstream: The Hirsel Country Park @Margaret Freeman; Crathie: Crathie Kirk @Roger Walton; page 194: Crieff: Glenturret: @Famous Grouse Experience; page 195: Cumnock: Dumfries House @The Great Steward of Scotland's Dumfries House Trust; pages 196 and 197: Edinburgh: Holyrood House @Simon Q; William and Kate @OIC Photos; St Giles' Cathedral @Veronika Kallus; page 198: Faslane: HM Naval Base Clyde @Crown Copyright 2015; page 199: Glasgow: Emirates Arena and Donald Dewar Leisure Centre @Glasgow Life, William @OIC Photos; page 200: Kelso: St Andrew's Episcopal Church @St Andrew's Episcopal Church; pages 201 and 202: St Andrews: William and Kate @OIC Photos; St Andrews @University of St Andrews; 13a Hope Street @Stephen Gibson; Hotel du Vin @Hotel du Vin; Balgove Farmhouse @Stephen Gibson.

INDEX